THE WALL STREET JOURNAL.

GUIDE TO
BUILDING YOUR
CAREER

THE WALL STREET JOURNAL.

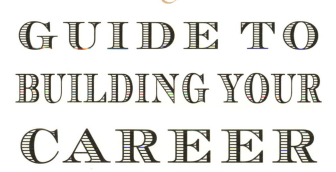

GUIDE TO BUILDING YOUR CAREER

JENNIFER MERRITT

CROWN
BUSINESS
NEW YORK

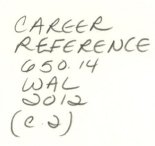

Copyright © 2012 by Dow Jones & Company, Inc.

The Wall Street Journal® is a registered trademark of Dow Jones and is used by permission.
All rights reserved.

Published in the United States by Crown Business, an imprint of the Crown Publishing Group, a division of Random House, Inc., New York.
www.crownpublishing.com

CROWN BUSINESS is a trademark and CROWN and the Rising Sun colophon are registered trademarks of Random House, Inc.

Crown business books are available at special discounts for bulk purchases for sales promotions or corporate use. Special editions, including personalized covers, excerpts of existing books, or books with corporate logos, can be created in large quantities for special needs. For more information, contact Premium Sales at (212) 572-2232 or e-mail specialmarkets@randomhouse.com.

Cataloging-in-Publication Data is on file with the Library of Congress.

ISBN 978-0-307-71956-0
eISBN 978-0-307-71957-7
Printed in the United States of America

Book design: Mauna Eichner and Lee Fukui
Cover illustration: © Peter Hoey/theispot.com

10 9 8 7 6 5 4 3 2 1

First Edition

CONTENTS

THE WALL STREET JOURNAL.

GUIDE TO BUILDING YOUR CAREER

You don't wait for opportunities, you make them come to you . . .

CHAPTER 1

WHAT IS A PROFESSIONAL CAREER?

This isn't just another book about how to get a job. Even in a tough economy, pretty much anyone can get some sort of job or another. No, this is a book about building a *career*. So, what *is* the difference between a job and a career? Simply put, a career is a lifelong endeavor, the pursuit of a professional track that consists of multiple jobs you'll stack one on top of the other (experts call it a career ladder for a reason), each tapping into skills and experiences you've already had and each adding a new set of skills, increased responsibilities and challenges, and fresh experiences.

For someone focused on a professional career track, each job you choose matters, so it's critical to consider not just what you can do in the next job, but also the tangible skills and experiences you can take away from each position and use for selling yourself in the future, says career coach J.T. O'Donnell of Careerealism.com. Figuring out what those skills are before you take a job is an art, of sorts, one that takes a few hits and even some misses to refine. But building a professional career is about landing the next job on the ladder—and you can do that only if you've built new skills each step of the way.

For the purposes of this guide, consider a professional career as one where you start in that ubiquitous entry-level position and climb the ladder toward a management or leadership position. How you get to that leadership role can vary—from a straight-line ladder leading up, to a zigzag climb that will find you moving among different functions or departments, sometimes moving laterally, then up, sometimes moving up a few rungs at a time. For many people, the path will be a bit of both.

Along the way, each job you choose should build the skills and experiences you need in order to reach your short-term and longer-term goals—starting as early as a strong internship in college (better yet, two) to help you land that first job after college.

I know it sounds daunting, but it doesn't have to be. This book will guide you through the steps you need to take, from deciding on a career path, to scoring that first internship, to making the most of it to pave the way to your first real job (don't worry, if you've already missed the internship boat, you can still get where you want to go with a little extra maneuvering you'll learn about in the following chapters). Then we'll look at how to land that first job, negotiate your first salary (which is crucial, as it's the starting place for all future salaries), and earn that critical early promotion that will put you on the path you desire. Then you'll learn some tricks for how to move up that ladder faster, including networking, smart early job moves that will set the foundation for your future success, career boosters that can set you apart from the crowd, and more.

WHERE TO START: DECIDING WHAT CAREER IS RIGHT FOR YOU

Many ambitious college students walk into their first class with a good idea about what they'd like to do when they "grow up," or at least a sense of the field they'd like to work in once

THE FASTEST GROWING PROFESSIONAL JOBS OR THE MOST NEW JOBS THROUGH 2018

Job	Growth (percent)	Number of new jobs (thousands)	Median wage (May 2008)	Education needed
Biomedical Engineer	72 percent	11.6	$77,400	Bachelor's degree
Network Systems/ Data Communications Analyst	53	115.8	71,100	Bachelor's
Financial Examiners	41	11.1	70,930	Bachelor's
Medical Scientists	40	44.2	72,950	Master's or Doctorate
Physician Assistants	39	29.2	81,230	Master's
Computer Software Engineers (Apps)	34	175.1	85,430	Bachelor's
Compliance Officers	31	80.8	48,890	Bachelor's
Accountants and Auditors	22	279.4	59,430	Bachelor's
Management Analysts	24	178.3	73,750	Bachelor's or higher
Financial Analysts	20	50.0	73,670	Bachelor's or higher
Civil Engineers	24	67.6	74,600	Bachelor's or higher
Market Research Analysts	28	70.1	61,070	Bachelor's or higher
Public Relations Specialists	24	66.2	51,280	Bachelor's
Financial Manager/ Banking	11	52.9	Varies by job	Bachelor's

Source: The Bureau of Labor Statistics' Occupational Outlook Handbook 2008–2018

they graduate. But that's just a start. Many industries and professions have become so diversified and segmented that simply saying you want to work in such-and-such field doesn't paint a full picture of what you really want to do.

Let's take engineering, for example. There are some two dozen specialties in engineering, from the more common civil, mechanical, chemical, and electrical, to the more specialized subsets such as aerospace, geotechnical, biomedical, environmental, petroleum, and nuclear. But even careers with fewer head-spinning options still present forks in the road. Take marketing: market research, promotions, account management, and even public relations and advertising can fall under the marketing moniker at many companies. The point is that before you decide which first job or internship to go after, you need to narrow down (as best you can) what *exactly* you ultimately want to do.

Of course, that's easier said than done. With all the different options out there, how are you supposed to figure out what field or industry most interests you? Well, it isn't easy, but the good news is, there's no wrong answer (although choosing a professional track that's not likely to be around in a decade might not be so wise). The key is to figure out the intersection between your interests and your aptitude. It helps to first rule out areas where what fascinates you does not match your abilities. For example, you might find biomedical engineering fascinating but struggle in biology classes. Or you might be drawn to market research but lack an aptitude for the database mining and analysis it actually requires. While there may be a sign that a particular job isn't right for you, a fascination with marketing might yield a more creative career in the field, or struggling in biology but not other earth sciences could make environmental engineering right for you.

At the end of the day, you aren't going to shine in a career if it's not something you've got both an aptitude and a passion for. Trust me, if you've got an aptitude for math and statistical analysis but can't stand the idea of running numbers be-hind the scenes and without a lot of people, being a financial analyst may not be for you. But you could put that aptitude to use elsewhere. The key to building a professional career starts with finding the proverbial sweet spot between what you do well and what you love to do.

Here are four questions—and strategies to help you find the answers—that will help you figure out the career that is right for you.

1. WHAT AM I BOTH GOOD AT AND FASCINATED BY?

If you've found yourself scoring A's in every history class you take, it could be because you're enthralled by the subject or that you're just really good at understanding historical con-text and writing papers that convey clear, concise, and persua-sive arguments. Both of those characteristics are critical for a career, be it history-related or not. Understanding the con-text of the projects you work on and being able to persuade with strong communication can go well beyond, say, becom-ing an historian at a local museum or a history teacher at a local college. So, think about the classes you've taken where you've both received strong grades and felt excited to attend (even if it was at the dreaded hour of 8:30 a.m.). They don't need to be classes only in your major, and you should con-sider extracurricular activities you love, too (after all, intra-mural soccer requires skills like teamwork, stamina, and mental agility; volunteering at a local senior center requires patience and empathy).

Once you've got a list of things that both hit the success button and have a strong happy factor, think about the skills you use when you're in those classes or participating in those activities. Consider both the tangible stuff—like strong writing or the know-how required to work through formulas—and the harder to quantify, such as deductive reasoning, connecting the dots to solve a problem, persuasion, team-building, or

CAREER POSSIBILITIES

What if you have no idea what you want to do? Here are some career paths within just two popular fields. You'll see the possibilities are numerous. For other careers, check out websites like WetFeet.com, Vault.com, and Quint Careers.com.

Finance

Commercial banking. Provide financial services for individuals and businesses (jobs include credit analyst, loan officer, trust officer, mortgage banker).

Investment banking. Assist companies, organizations, governments, and sometimes individuals in raising money through issuing of securities; deal with mergers and acquisitions; handles IPOs, etc. (jobs include equity research, corporate finance analyst, equities trader, ratings analyst, broker).

Money management. Decide on, hold, and help trade stocks and bonds for institutions or individuals (jobs include portfolio manager, hedge fund analyst or trader, financial advisor, mutual fund analyst; for individuals, financial planner).

Corporate finance. Work inside a company to help find money to maintain and grow the business, make acquisitions, or manage cash and investments (jobs include credit manager, treasurer, financial analyst, investor relations, controller, credit analyst, financial strategist).

Insurance. Help companies or individuals manage risk to protect from losses (jobs include agent, broker, actuary, risk manager, underwriter, loss control, claims adjuster, sales).

Real estate. Handle the money side of real estate transactions and development from mortgages to title insurance to real estate investment, management, and development (jobs include commercial sales, appraiser, business development, financial analyst).

Marketing—Either Through an Agency or Internally

(Keep in mind, these paths can be taken in a variety of fields; you could do market research in any industry, from accounting to high technology to pharmaceuticals and more.)

Account management. Following and managing client accounts or marketing projects from beginning to end (jobs include account coordinator, account executive, account specialist).

Market research. Analyze data and trends to determine the need, desire, pricing, etc., on products and services (jobs include researcher, market analyst, marketing data strategist).

Promotions. Get the word out and build enthusiasm for products through sweepstakes, samples, rebates, coupons, and other programs (jobs include promotion coordinator, promotions manager, promotion strategist).

Communications/strategy. Developing targeted or mass messaging to manage and build a brand (jobs include social media manager, social media strategist, marketing communications manager, crisis communications strategist).

creating new formulas or ideas. Write down these skills you employ and then weight them. No, it's not a grading curve—just another critical-thinking exercise that will force you to really think about what you're good at. Number the five skills you feel you most excel in, with the standout skill as No. 1. If you aren't sure about which skills you're using or what you're best at, quiz professors or classmates who know you well to help round out your own thinking.

You can also see if your university offers workshops directly linked to—or based on—the Dependable Strengths Articulation Process program. You'll sit with a small group of students and go through a series of exercises that help discern your strengths. From conversations about your best experiences and your not-so-great experiences, the people in your group record the strengths they think you're describing—and you'll do the same for them. There'll be a gut-check about how valid those strengths are, and in the end, you'll be able to match those strengths with various career paths.[1] Sounds a little kumbaya, for sure, but the process has been around for more than fifty years and can be wildly helpful for driven—but uncertain—professionals and early careerists.

At many colleges and universities, you can also tap peer advisors—often through the career services office—who've been there, done that and who get a little extra training to help other students wade through the process of the right fit for their skills and interests. Some even maintain regular blogs or daily newsletters to offer advice, give feedback, and share their own experiences selecting a career or landing an internship. You can often read these even if you aren't a student. One particularly helpful one: the University of California–Berkeley's Peer Corner blog, which offers advice and insights from students from a variety of majors.[2]

2. How can I translate that into a job in my chosen field?

You've got your list. And you're pretty sure it serves to confirm your desire to build a career in banking. Or maybe you've realized you'd really be excited by a career managing a brand or developing new consumer product launches. Or your list is so problem-solver heavy that it's clear that consulting is right for you. Now it's gut-check time. Make an appointment with the career services office or peer advisor group at your college and go over your list of skills and your career attractions. These professionals might suggest a series of quizzes or questionnaires to help refine your list. They will also have a strong sense of where in your chosen field those skills will get you in the door—and off to a strong start.

As you shape the list of possibilities, consider what other classes you might need to take in order to round out the required skill set. If, say, it turns out that your penchant for visual thinking and your winning potato-chip campaign in the last marketing class you took make you a perfect candidate to move into branding or marketing for a big consumer goods company, that track will also involve some quantitative knowledge to help you understand concepts like budgeting and market statistics. (You'll want to look for courses to round out those skills, if you don't already have them.)

3. WHAT'S IT REALLY LIKE TO DO THOSE JOBS?

Don't leave the career office just yet. Ask if yours keeps a database of recent graduates and more-experienced alumni who are willing to connect with students interested in similar career paths; most schools do and they've been aggressive in the last few years about updating those lists and making inroads with alums on behalf of job-seeking students. Ask for a list of alumni you can reach out to. Check with your parents, professors, and family friends for a similar list. Make the connection with a simple phone call or an e-mail. Introduce yourself—and the person who referred you—and quickly acknowledge that you know this person's time is valuable, but that you hope he could spend fifteen minutes in the next week or two telling you about his job.

When you chat, ask about a typical day, the next-step jobs your new contact is pursuing, and what those are like (after all, you might want to follow his path), and ask what skills are most critical to get started on the same path. Be sure to ask about the personality types that fit best in the career and the positions your contact has had. You might love the idea of being a junior trader on a stock or commodity exchange, but if you're the cooperative, teamwork type, you'll find you don't have the sharp elbows and a tough-as-nails personality the job might require.

Take careful notes. If you find yourself even more interested—and your contact is nearby and seems enthusiastic about taking you under his wing—ask if you might shadow him for a day. And don't be lackadaisical with your efforts; even if the first person you reach gives you plenty of time and insight, it's important to speak with at least three or four people already pursuing each path you're interested in. Each person will add a little something to your thinking process.

4. CAN I TRY THIS OUT FOR A DAY?

Now you've got a pretty good idea of what you want to do. Next up: Ask career services about externships—experiential learning opportunities, similar to internships, but usually lasting a day to a few days, that are designed to give students a flavor of a career in the path that interests them. Unlike an internship, the goal here is to further explore a career, not to get actual experience. A number of universities have set up extensive programs to make externships possible. (Cornell University, for example, has a broad-based extern program that gives students a chance to apply to shadow experienced Cornell alumni over winter break as early as sophomore year—and another spring-break job-shadowing program for freshmen. Many schools, from the elite to public state institutions, offer something similar.) Take advantage of these recent opportunities.

Individual company career portals often have information about such opportunities; of course you can also ask the alumni contacts you've spoken to. Most externships will involve a day or two of shadowing a midlevel professional in the careers you're interested in. In some cases, you can extern for a day or two with several different people in different companies and fields. Often, consulting, accounting, and finance firms—and sometimes engineering concerns—will host their own externships. You'll need to search the career websites of individual companies for instructions on applying or look for a list at your career services office.

ABOUT THOSE ALUMNI

Hire education blogger (blogs.wsj.com/hire-education) Shalini Sharan, then a senior economics major at Bates College, wrote about her experiences reaching out and finding information about work and internships:

"I was initially hesitant to contact them, but it was easier once I got past the awkwardness and realized that they have all been in my shoes before. I sent out scores of e-mails to alumni working in fields like consulting and research and managed to hear back from most of them. E-mails were followed by phone conversations that helped me immensely in figuring out my summer plans. While these conversations didn't directly translate into an internship, I made some valuable connections that helped me understand the nature of the jobs I was inquiring about. To be honest, I was looking for any opportunity that could fill an otherwise futile summer, but in the process, I learned where my interests really lie.

"In many cases—especially if there aren't many options to be found at your school or too-few recruiters in the fields you are interested in visiting your campus—the career portals of the companies you're interested in working for are among the best places to get comprehensive information about internships. If you want to, say, get an internship at an accounting firm, go to the career websites of the twenty-five largest firms (you can find a list at your career service office or online) and you'll undoubtedly find information on internship programs. The same is true in many fields." [3]

Another option: be bold, contact a local company, and ask about shadowing an employee or group. Before making that call, research the firm and be ready to offer suggestions about the group, team, or person you'd be most interested in shadowing. You can also contact professional associations most related to the career field you're considering. They'll often offer workshops, seminars, or handouts on what the field is really like and might be able to point you to shadowing opportunities that you might not find elsewhere.

Whatever you do, don't miss out on the opportunity to ask questions of the person you follow for the day. You're making an educated decision about your future and you can't do it without arming yourself with firsthand information, insight, and advice. Thank the person you've shadowed or externed with in person and with a follow-up e-mail or note. While a day or two of shadowing won't tell you all you need to know about working in a specific job or career field, you will get a good feel for the type of tasks you'd be handling and the sort of environment you'd be working in every day. What's more, the contacts you make are sure to be valuable down the road.

Some externships are actually much more structured and involve real work. For example, in late 2010, George Washington University senior Ashley Starks participated in Deloitte Consulting's federal consulting externship. The externship was a two-day case competition where thirty undergraduate students were introduced to Strategy and Operations Federal Practice Consulting. Case competition materials were handed out and the students divided into teams with just over a day to develop a case to present to senior leaders at the firm. And the students had the opportunity to talk with consultants at every level in the firm and have lunch with firm leaders. Each team's work analyzing the case they were handed ended with a presentation to those executives, followed by feedback about their performance.[4]

Ashley walked away with an understanding of the culture and goal-oriented atmosphere at the consulting firm and with insight into the challenges of implementing policy and executive orders as a consultant. By taking advantage of the time she had to talk with consultants and firm executives, Ashley also was able to map out the various career paths and skills she'd need to succeed in the industry. What's more, the fast pace and level of analysis required—and the desire to impress the execs she was presenting to and chatting with—gave Ashley a clearer view of her strengths and the areas where she needed to learn more and grow. [5]

CHAPTER 2

THE INTERNSHIP IS THE NEW FIRST JOB

Wait, don't you have until senior year in college to start the big first-job hunt? Maybe your older sister who graduated in 2005 got away with putting off a serious job hunt until after graduation and still landed well, but not anymore.

These days, it's critical to have at least one meaningful internship during college (maybe even two) in order to land that first job post-graduation. In a 2010 survey of more than 420 recruiters by *The Wall Street Journal*, 25 percent reported that *more than half* of their newly minted college graduate hires had been interns at the company; some said more than 80 percent of new hires were once interns at the company. As companies have become more thinly staffed, internships have become their way of test-driving potential hires. These days, it's crucial to get serious about a career track earlier, and gain some experience in demanding professional settings well before it's time to don a cap and gown. Call it the new normal of career-building.

Remember that stat—some 25 percent of 420 recruiters said more than half of their new-grad hires first had internships with their companies? Well, those companies altogether hired more than 43,000 new graduates between spring 2009 and spring 2010. What's more, a full 14 percent actually reported that at least three out of four (75 percent) of their new-grad hires had been interns. And those are just the people who accepted offers. Many of those same companies say they offered jobs to a significantly higher percentage of their interns. Want more proof that a successful internship is critical? The National Association of Colleges and Employers (NACE) reported in its 2010 Internship and Co-op Survey that nearly 57 percent of students from the class of 2009 were converted from interns to full-time hires, up from 50 percent the previous year.[6]

A diploma from a prestigious university used to be enough to get on the career ladder. But over the last several years, strong performance in solid internships has really become the key factor—aside from education—that sets apart the successful future professional from the rest of the pack. The trend toward companies hiring largely from their intern pool has accelerated at warp speed in the past three to five years, according to Monica Wilson, acting co-director of career services at Dartmouth College. "Internship recruiting will largely replace entry-level recruiting in the next few years," she says. And her observation echoes what other career service administrators across the country are seeing and what dozens and dozens of recruiters have been saying for the last several years.

STARTING EARLIER AND OFFERING MORE

The importance of getting that internship as early as sophomore year of college has created a lot of pressure to decide on a career track sooner. But here's the good news: companies are also targeting and reaching out to students sooner; these days, even incoming freshmen are exposed to corporate presentations and meet-and-greets with recruiters, sometimes within just weeks of arriving on campus. Accounting firm PricewaterhouseCoopers, for example, holds information sessions almost as soon as classes start and makes internship offers to rising juniors and seniors as early as the last week of September. Case in point: the firm hired 1,454 rising juniors and seniors for summer 2010 internships and offered 90 percent of eligible interns a full-time position before they returned to campus.[7]

Why is all this good news? For starters, this early interest from employers means you'll be exposed much earlier to various companies, career paths, and real hands-on work in internships than your counterparts who graduated a decade ago. You might even land a professional internship that will set you on your career path as early as the summer after your freshman year. Think about it. If you complete two strong internships, you'll have as much practical experience at graduation as someone six to twelve months into their first job might have had even five or six years ago. But that's only going to be the case if you make your own "luck" by using each corporate meet-and-greet and internship as another building block or two for your professional career (more on creating your own luck later).

It really wasn't long ago that an internship (with some exceptions in highly competitive fields) didn't offer much in the way of meaningful work or valuable experience. Worst case: you'd be making coffee and filing, or doing other mostly mundane tasks. Best case: maybe you'd be able to contribute at the margins by assisting on a project or helping a consultant prepare a presentation. If you were really lucky, you might even be invited to a brainstorming session. But it was almost unheard of to actually be handed a project to tackle yourself or be expected to function like a real employee or core team member. Well, not anymore.

INTERNSHIP AS RECRUITING TOOL

Companies like General Electric, Pricewaterhouse, NetApp, and Boeing (the aerospace company reported that 28 percent of its new-grad job offers were to former interns in 2010, a number company officials expect to rise) say they have gone to great lengths in the last several years to treat their interns like real employees, offering interns deeper work experiences, real responsibility, and meaningful assignments, and even measuring interns' work in the same way they measure the progress of full-time staff. It's all part of an effort to test-drive potential future employees in a situation where the stakes are lower for the firm and where managers still have a close eye on progress and performance. Among employers responding to the National Association of College Employers 2010 Internship and Co-op Survey, 84 percent say internship programs are designed to help the organization recruit entry-level college hires.

At Chicago-based Boeing Co., Katrina Krebs, who in the summer of 2010 was a rising junior at University of Washington, helped solve a noise-complaint problem with partitions on 777 planes. For two weeks, Ms. Krebs pulled aircraft plans and met with senior design engineers and mechanics to disassemble the partition before she and a manager brainstormed possible design solutions. She presented the possible solution that was eventually adopted and she got to work with another team to implement the fix. "We do everything we can to facilitate meaningful work assignments for interns," said Bud Fishback, who manages college intern programs for Boeing.

Even if you decide not to go back to the firm where you interned, that tangible experience will be valuable in your full-time job search and could even set you apart from graduates who had less-meaningful internship experiences.

The most recent National Association of Colleges and Employers survey of new college grads (conducted in 2010) revealed that new grads with internship experience were "considerably more likely to receive a job offer" than other 2010 graduates who didn't have an internship under their belt. About 42 percent of graduates with internships "who applied for a job received an offer compared with only 30 percent for students who had no internship experience."

Need more proof that the pressure to intern is actually good news? People who have completed internships get paid more, too. The NACE study found that graduates with internships received a "significantly higher starting salary offer." Grads with previous internship experience received a median starting salary of $41,580; those without an internship on their résumé got median offers of $34,601.[8]

CHOOSING A CAREER-LAUNCHING INTERNSHIP

First things first: never accept an internship that doesn't offer tangible, hands-on, practical experience. You need that to build your résumé—and, in interviews for full-time posts later, to be able to tout what you've actually done (not just where you've interned, which no longer cuts it). If you end up with a full-time job offer from the company you interned with, it will be how you met or exceeded expectations in those tasks—along with the company's assessment of how well you fit in at the firm—during the summer that will set you apart from your peers (you know, the ones who did good work, but didn't get an offer before they returned to campus). What's more, even if a company offers you a permanent spot before you leave for the summer—which happens most in fields like accounting, engineering, and technology—you might decide not to take it after you see what the work is like.

It's true that a big-name firm might make for the "right" name on a résumé—helpful for sure—but it's more important to make sure the internship accomplishes the following:

1. takes advantage of the skills you have and the education you've received;

2. helps you build new skills and competencies;

3. provides meaningful work (the sort where you can later tell an interviewer something like "I worked on a ten-million-dollar project for an international

client and was part of a team responsible for analyzing the new business opportunities for the firm in three new countries in Asia" or "I worked side-by-side with a CPA auditing a two-billion-dollar client's books and spotted three trouble spots that saved the company money");

4. offers exposure to key managers and executives (don't expect lunch with the CEO, but if you sit in meetings with a regional director, division manager, assistant vice president, or other senior managers who report to those people, consider yourself exposed); and

5. could lead to a full-time job later (some companies explain up front that an internship is a foot in the door, while others will tell you they don't hire directly from the new college grad pool but will consider you with a few years of experience).

While it shouldn't be a deal-breaker, you should also look for internships that have a dedicated internship coordinator or an intern mentor program. The intern coordinator or assigned mentor will be charged with making sure your internship stays on track and can be a valuable resource during the summer. What's more, these folks often hold weight with hiring managers—after all, they've seen hundreds of eager interns over the years, and standing out with them means a lot—and could turn into critical contacts when you're looking for full-time work. Having a go-to contact is particularly important for internships that include a start-to-finish project that results in a presentation or report. That's partly because you might be left largely on your own from time to time; if you get stuck or concerned about the direction you're headed, a mentor or intern supervisor can often provide an indirect line to assistance and serve as a sounding board before you go to the boss for help (finding answers yourself is a key way to stand out during an internship).

These days, most big companies do offer such internships. But if you want to work at a midsize or smaller company, the structure and depth of the internship might be spottier. You might have to take much more initiative (that's a plus, more on how to do that in a few pages) to help the firm create a meaningful internship for you. To find out which companies hire from your school and offer in-depth internships, start with your college or university career services office and other students who have had internships in previous summers.

You should also attend the presentations of companies that come to campus—but be selective, spend your time at the presentations from firms you'd most like to work for in the field you've zoomed in on. One tip: go to these presentations fully prepared. Research the firm and its businesses and ask former interns about their experiences. The reason? Many such corporate presentations turn into impromptu internship screenings. Be prepared to participate if you're asked!

STANDING OUT TO LAND THE INTERNSHIP

Here's a daunting scenario: You show up for a corporate presentation where you know they'll be doing internship screening . . . and so do two hundred of your classmates. You've just learned that landing good internships is critical to launching your career. So how on earth can you stand out from that kind of crowd? Well, here's something you might not realize: you likely know just as much as those classmates, and you can make sure that potential employer knows it by following a few easy steps.

For starters, the depth of your company research can be a huge plus. Before you set foot into the presentation room, you should know the basics of the company's business, its areas of growth, and some of its recent key initiatives. If your career services office has reviews from former interns, read up. And if those alumni contacts you made when you were narrowing your career-fit worked at the firm, ring them up for a follow-up about the firm itself. Then, when it's your turn to chat with a representative, don't be shy. Politely discuss the business initiatives and other aspects of the firm that spark your interest—just don't force the conversation. For example, when asked, "What interests you about Big Widget?" you might say, "I'm really dedicated to pursuing a career in the widget field because of the constant innovation and challenges. Big Widget has been on the leading edge of so much of that, what with its ultra-Widget project and the initiative to get widgets into third-world countries. I know that classmates who have interned at the firm say that it's a great place to work, too, especially for people who've got a keen interest in widget-tech. I've been doing side projects in that since I was a teenager and even did a freshman project on the topic." Voilà: you've proven you're truly interested by relating your personal interests and knowledge to the firm's, that you've taken the time to find out about how the firm operates, both culturally and within the marketplace, that you have real reasons for targeting this firm in particular, and that you know about the company and its big initiatives.

Believe it or not, company reps say too few students bother to do this, which means you'll stand out simply for making half as elaborate an effort—doubly so if you demonstrate that you've given some thought to what the firm does and how you might fit in. If you don't feel excited about the company or the prospect of interning in one of its departments, you're better off skipping the presentation and interview process altogether—it will be obvious to the interviewer. Remember, some 30 percent of hiring managers will decide whether to make you an offer within fifteen minutes of meeting you, according to research from the Society of Human

Resource Management. First impressions really are as important as your mom and dad have said they are.

The same goes for a formal interview. Enthusiasm is critical. And so is that homework. In many cases, you won't have much work experience to discuss, but before you go to an interview, figure out what experiences you can translate into interview speak. For example, if you were a summer camp counselor for three years in a row, the last year in a leadership role over other counselors and campers, mention your sense of commitment to work you love and your ability to take on significant responsibility. Examples of taking initiative or solving problems on your own in former jobs or volunteer roles can also be strong evidence of your internship-readiness. If you work part-time during the school year, work in the idea that you are able to balance a demanding school schedule and a job. If you've assisted a professor with research related to the field you're pursuing, you should be prepared to discuss what you did and detail the tangible results of your work. Have these examples in mind—jot them down in the days leading up to an interview and refresh your memory a few hours prior to your meeting—and look for ways to work them into the conversation or use them as answers to questions. Remember, confidence begets confidence, so walk and talk the part and prepare to stand out.

While a few fields, such as government and electronics, have increased the number of internship positions this school year, other industries, such as finance and engineering, have seen the number of available internships drop. And while according to surveys by NACE, there was an expected 3 percent uptick in intern hiring for summer 2011 over 2010—on top of a 2.9 percent increase in 2010 over 2009—that doesn't come close to making up for the 20 percent drop experienced between the summers of 2008 and 2009.

Those stats, combined with the fact that you might not *want* to work for a traditional big company, makes networking and approaching small and midsize companies with

CREATING YOUR OWN INTERNSHIP

For some people, a traditional internship just won't do. If your aspirations don't fit into a preset internship or you happen to be internship-hunting during a time when employers are cutting back on summer hires, you can create your own internship.

"There's no cookie-cutter approach to building your own internship," Richard Bottner, president of Intern Bridge, an internship consulting and research firm in Acton, Massachusetts, told *The Wall Street Journal*. "It's about getting out there and networking."[9]

Usually, creating your own internship means approaching small and midsize companies with a pitch—and a big dose of eagerness. Make a list of target companies or organizations you'd like to work for and research them to find out who heads the department you'd most like to work in.

Mr. Bottner recommends joining a professional association tied to your industry as a way to meet people at the companies you'd like to work for who can connect you with hiring managers or help you set up informational interviews. If you don't know anyone in the business, meet with alumni from your university who work there. You can also connect with someone on LinkedIn.com or, as a last resort, contact the company's human resources department, he says.

Then, send a note expressing your interest in working with the company over the summer. Your note should detail exactly how you believe you can contribute to the firm—and just a few sentences about what you hope to gain. The key is to pitch your skill set, your eagerness, and your ability to help the company—and learn at the same time.

Before making your pitch, be sure to research the company and tailor your proposal to focus on how your skills will improve its business. Show the company how what you're offering will help it stretch its dollars or increase revenue, says Colleen Sabatino, a career counselor and intern coach for Internships.com, which helps students land internships.

Keep in mind that many times such internships are unpaid or come with only a small stipend. Some colleges and universities have funds for students who take unpaid summer jobs or who create their own internships. In other cases, you can ask for and receive college credit for the work.

If you land a self-created internship, be sure to meet with your summer boss to lay out what he hopes you'll accomplish while you are there—and what you hope to learn. It will be incumbent on you to make sure you build some skills and get the kind of experience you need to land a job later.

enthusiasm and a plan in hand a good way to get the work experience you need on your résumé to land a job after graduation. Richard Bottner says there's no one approach to building your own internship, but it can be done.

If you're set on creating your own internship, networking is key. Start by joining a professional association tied to your industry as a way to meet people at the companies where you'd like to work. It's those folks who are most likely to be able to connect you with hiring managers or help you set up informational interviews. If you don't know anyone in the business or can't easily join an association, contact alumni from your university who work at the firm or firms you've got your heart set on. You can also try to connect with someone on LinkedIn.com or, as a last resort, contact the company's human resources department.

But, of course, you can't just call and ask for an internship. You'll have to make a persuasive pitch. To do that, first be sure to research the company and tailor your proposal to focus on how your skills will improve the business. Hone in on areas where the company is growing or on initiatives you've read about in the news or on the company's website. Show the decision makers how what you're offering will help them stretch their dollars or increase revenue. And where possible, let your status as a student work for you.

If you're a marketing major, you could offer to work with the marketing team to develop a strategy to reach college kids with a new product or service. Or if your plan is to work in business operations, consider pitching an internship that lets you try to apply the latest operations concepts and strategies to the firm's business or new initiatives—to see if the latest Ivory Tower concepts really do work. In a case like that, you might even be able to get credit for the internship. Outline—loosely—what you might do each week or month, what you expect to deliver in the end, and how you see what you bring to the internship as a benefit to the firm. Your pitch should be one to two pages and be professionally written (any doubts, ask someone in career services to read over your pitch; there may even be a template to follow).

The bottom line: Pitch your skill set and recent or cutting-edge knowledge as it applies to the firm. Bounce your idea off the contacts you've made at the firm and refine your pitch with that person's help. Best case, they'll be impressed and usher your pitch to the higher-ups. But if that doesn't happen, ask to be directed to the person you'd most likely work for in this self-created internship and ask for an introduction so you can make your pitch.

You might be surprised to find that small companies in particular will be open to your pitch. "It's a good opportunity for small-business owners," Keith Ashmus, chair of the National Small Business Association and a cofounding partner at Frantz Ward LLP, a law firm in Cleveland, told *The Wall Street Journal*.[10] The reason, he and others say: interns can help out on projects that might not otherwise get done and they can also help to energize a team with their enthusiasm. What's more, for smaller firms losing out on full-time hires to bigger competitors, it's a chance to win you over for the future.

Now, you might be wondering, am I going to get paid for this? The answer might be no. But an increasing number of schools are offering funding to students who self-create internships. Check with your career services office to find out what your school offers. Syracuse University, for example, offers internship awards, ranging from $2,500 to $5,000, for undergraduate and graduate students who design their own internships. You can also ask the firm you've targeted if a small stipend is possible—say, $100 to $150 a week—to cover your commuting costs. Wait to ask until they say they're interested in your services. Another possibility: request that your internship be part-time; in that case you could find a paying job to supplement your bank account.

And keep in mind that there might be other rewards, aside from pay. For example, in 2007, Stephanie Gurtman was set on interning for Pyper Paul + Kenney, an advertising agency in her hometown of Tampa, Florida, the summer after her freshman year at Boston University. There didn't seem to be any advertised internships at the firm, so Stephanie requested an informational interview with the public-relations director while she was home on spring break.

At the meeting Stephanie pitched her writing skills and self-starter attitude and made it clear that she wanted to be involved in brainstorming sessions, client pitches, and off-site photo shoots. The firm created a position where she could do those things and also help to write and distribute press releases, conduct market research, and assemble press kits. The internship was unpaid, but she walked away with three letters of recommendation that helped her land future internships.[11]

ASK SMART QUESTIONS

During your internship interview, be sure to ask smart questions—and make mental note of the answers. Before the interview ends, make sure you ask about typical responsibilities of an intern and probe for details about the kind of projects or assignments you might receive. Find out how often interns are invited back, either for a second summer or for full-time jobs. Ask what common traits those who are asked back possess—if you land the internship, you'll want to be sure to emulate those traits, even if you later decide this particular employer is not a good fit for you.

IT'S JUNE. NOW WHAT?

It's Day One of your internship and you've already attended the orientation (arriving on time, of course), been directed to the manager you'll be reporting to, and shown your desk. Any minute now you'll get your first assignment (and if you don't, ask for one). Dun-dun-dun. Cue the deer-in-headlights feeling. You'll be wondering—even if you asked long ago—how, exactly, do I succeed in this internship? Don't worry if the answer doesn't come to you right away; it will. Tackle the summer internship like you would a class you love and want to ace—give the work your full attention, study up, and put your best work forward. Seems obvious, right?

The key to your success for the next eight to twelve weeks (the typical length of a summer internship) will be to exceed your boss's expectations. Doing so—and in the process building your skills and creating critical accomplishments to add to your résumé—is the first real step in building your professional career. Trust me on this one: as a journalist, my first internship at *BusinessWeek* magazine set the stage for the remainder of my career, both because of the depth of the responsibility I was given and also because I walked in with a can-do spirit, soaked up the expertise of the reporters and editors around me, asked for extra assignments, and had something to show for my work (four good story clips and a mention in a book) at the end of the summer. What's more, I impressed the boss, who became a lifelong mentor and reference and who asked me back to fill an opening on staff a few years later. I'm not alone. As careers editor, I heard and read countless stories of the lingering impact of a strong internship performance.

ACT THE PART

First off, behaving professionally is a given. What does that mean? Simply put: dress the part (look around at how full-time

THE GOLD STANDARD

A look at Goldman Sachs Do's and Don'ts for interns . . . [12]

The Do's

- ☐ Be eager for a challenge.
- ☐ Be yourself.
- ☐ Be open-minded.
- ☐ Be on time.
- ☐ Know the dress code.
- ☐ Observe and ask thoughtful questions.
- ☐ Treat everyone you meet with respect and professionalism.
- ☐ Understand that everyone makes mistakes.
- ☐ Carry a notebook with you at all times.
- ☐ Pay attention to the details.
- ☐ Be proactive.
- ☐ Show energy and interest.
- ☐ Set goals for yourself.

The Don'ts

- ☐ Let a bad day get you down.
- ☐ Take on more than you can handle.
- ☐ Pretend to know something you don't.
- ☐ Have nothing to do.
- ☐ Ask everyone the same questions.
- ☐ Take yourself too seriously.
- ☐ Talk negatively about coworkers.
- ☐ Focus all of your attention on senior management.

☐ Bring your personal life into the office.

☐ Surf the Web all day.

☐ Spend working hours on social networking sites or texting friends.

staffers are dressed and try to emulate them); speak clearly; show up for work on time—a few minutes early is best; don't skip meetings or anything else you're requested, or even invited, to attend; meet your deadlines with room to spare (sorry, no handing in your work one minute before the boss hits the exit for the day); if you have questions, ask them at the right time (when the boss or a colleague is available and able to answer, not after you've already guessed yourself); and when writing memos or e-mails, use proper grammar and avoid falling into casual, or worse, text message language (signing your e-mails "thx" or "thnk u" is not going to fly).

A dose of humility mixed in with your enthusiasm and ambition is also important. Don't take it upon yourself to add extra touches to a presentation or to answer a tricky client question without permission or a full understanding of the issues. But do politely suggest an idea or answer—or offer to find one—to the boss or the person running the project. And, as unpleasant as it might be, if you're asked to do a few menial tasks, just do them. Don't grumble (even under your breath).

It doesn't matter how good of a college you go to or how overqualified or overeducated you may be to perform these mundane tasks; if you're an intern, you're at the bottom of the totem pole, and you have to pay your dues. Complaining about it is not only unprofessional, and will make the internship experience that much less satisfying for you. In an internship, where your goal is to make a good impression, learn all you can, enhance your skills, and build your résumé; the small stuff matters. So, do that filing or binder-making with a smile, knowing that showing competency in the little things almost always leads to less grunt work and more responsibility, even in the short span of a summer.

Here's another tip. While there's nothing wrong with asking for help or guidance, you'll stand out—and prove something about your critical thinking and potential—if you don't head straight to the boss for answers, but instead consult with a peer, intern supervisor, or mentor first. Better yet, find the answer yourself using the resources at your disposal—like a company database or a quick review of similar projects the firm has done before. Questions are good. And bosses are open to them. But self-sufficiency means finding other resources to answer questions outside of clarifications about the actual assignment. In many instances, you can solve small problems or find the answers to more basic questions without going to the boss. Later, you can briefly explain that you weren't sure about the answer to X, but after looking through the data set and consulting with a colleague, you discovered Y. A boss will appreciate your initiative and see you're able to work independently. And you'll be able to work more efficiently on the tasks you are assigned because you won't need to run to the boss at every turn.

A few years ago I spoke to a woman whose story drives home this point. As a civil engineering student she was working with a department of transportation contractor charged with inspecting bridges. She had plenty of technical know-how. But she'd never actually inspected an entire bridge and really wasn't sure she had a grasp of the big picture at an actual work site. Her solution? She donned a hard hat, climbed to the highest point overlooking the site, and observed. She took notes on what she saw (even detailing what the different crew leaders were wearing, since she didn't yet know their names), jotted down who did what, and watched the processes in place.

The intern knew she'd be analyzing the results of that day's work during her inspections, and understanding how the pieces fit, she surmised, would be one way to understand how her actions might impact the rest of the work site. Regarding anything she didn't understand, she'd find the person she had described in her notes and ask. All the while, she never bothered her supervisor until she had a question that stumped her. Later that summer, the boss recalled her first days. He'd been impressed with her initiative and had noticed her effort to figure out what the heck she was supposed to be doing. His reference and support proved to be key in landing a scholarship the following semester and in securing a job later.

Another way to avoid looking unprofessional or greener than you really are: avoid saying things like "In class, we did X and Y." It will remind people you are merely an intern; in most cases, you'll be better off pausing for a moment to consider how the concepts you picked up in class or in a particular project or experiment can be applied to the task you're involved with now. It's much better to be able to present an idea as a "what if we tried this" or "what if we did that" rather than to just talk about a similar scenario tested in the safe confines of a classroom or school lab. What's more, showing you aren't just smart but also that you can *apply* what you know will stick with your supervisor when it comes time to hand out higher-stakes assignments or write intern reviews.

GET DIRECTION AND SEEK FEEDBACK

Of course, before you can wow, you've got to have a good idea of what you're supposed to be doing. In some internships responsibilities are very clearly defined (Katrina Krebs, who interned with Boeing, for example, was given several clear assignments all lasting about a month, that were partly independent and partly collaborative; consultancies often give interns key pieces of a project to manage under a senior consultant, with due dates, specific goals, and exposure to clients at critical junctures). In some cases, a firm will have your direct supervisor hand out assignments. In that case, it's critical to meet regularly with her to discuss whether you are meeting expectations and to get feedback on your performance. And don't just set off on an assignment, ask for clarity on anything you don't fully understand before you get started.

And remember, you're interning to get something out of it, too. It's not all about the firm. Be sure to discuss your goals if your supervisor doesn't ask. And when you check in during the summer, revisit those goals. If you're meeting the boss's expectations, but not addressing some of the expectations you brought with you, suggest ways to do so that fit in with the team or company and its broader mandates.

Another great source of feedback and direction: the staffers and other interns you work alongside. Staffers are closer to where you are now—e.g., internships—than, say, a manager with two decades of work experience under her belt, and they might be more willing to take you under their wing and informally direct you or offer feedback and tips for working with the group or the boss. And your fellow interns might have received additional details or feedback about an assignment that can help all of you.

THE UNWRITTEN RULES OF THE OFFICE

In an episode of the hit television show *The Office,* Jim is made boss while Michael Scott, the actual boss, goes off to the wilderness to find himself. One of the first things Jim does as "boss" is to hastily eliminate the individual birthday celebrations that had been tradition in the office. After all, taking special orders for cake after cake is expensive, and wouldn't it be better to have a celebration for, say, every birthday in a month with bigger cakes, but fewer of them and fewer workday disruptions? Did someone say office mutiny? Exactly.

Office traditions and cultural norms are often unwritten and almost always sacred. More than most people will admit, the way people view you can often be clouded by how you respond to a firm or group's cultural norms. If you're doing stellar work but don't try to adapt, your internship won't be successful. If you adapt easily, you'll be remembered and appreciated (as long as your work is solid) even if another intern happens to have outpaced you by a smidge.

While you won't be faced with temporarily acting as the boss, you will be faced with a minefield of unwritten rules of office conduct. The best way to learn them is to be very observant. Make mental notes on everything in your first week or two on the job. How do people address each other—formally or more collegially? If it's a collegial environment, don't immediately assume you're one of the gang—watch to see how staffers interact with your fellow interns and gradually warm up to the friendliness. If everyone interacts more formally, with meetings scheduled days in advance and e-mails that start with "Dear So-and-So," you should model the same with your interactions. Watch to see how supervisors interact with the staffers they manage. Is he an e-mail-first-and-chat-when-needed type or someone who prefers regular in-person check-ins and updates? Observe how he interacts with those on staff for clues and try to copy those staffers, with an extra measure of deference. If people tend to keep to themselves, you do the same, at least at first. If everyone congregates at a set of picnic tables outside to eat lunch, ask if you can join in; if your group members eat lunch at their desks, do the same at least a few times a week. Other things to notice: Do people take turns making Starbucks runs every afternoon? After a few days on the job, offer to take a turn (and then be sure to get the orders on paper).

A final note on culture: observing the way things work in the company and department can be valuable for making your own decisions about where and how you want to work. If you find it off-putting that people in your group are sharp-elbowed or if you find yourself uncomfortable that the bosses offer only negative feedback as a standard practice, it's unlikely that you'll want to work at the firm after you graduate. A job is as much about cultural fit as it is about professional fit, and the two are closely related. If you're uncomfortable enough with the atmosphere of the office and the management style at a company, you're unlikely to do your very best work (and that's critical to finding your next, next job).

GOING ABOVE AND BEYOND— THE RIGHT WAY

There are two kinds of going above and beyond. The first: doing more than is expected in the work you're assigned. The easiest way to do that is to immerse yourself in your assignments and use your time wisely. Don't socialize too much and avoid gossip or getting involved in any office politics. Focus instead on going the extra mile on the work you've been assigned. That said, going above and beyond doesn't mean overdoing it. If you're asked to brainstorm and come up with two ideas for a marketing campaign for your employer's newest widget, it's not impressive if you come back with five ideas. Rather, doing so will likely send a message to the boss that you're unfocused and unable to think critically to suss out the two best ideas.

Instead, be decisive, narrow the ideas yourself, and then do a thorough job researching and supporting them. Don't just say that a television campaign aimed at teens and young adults is one of the best ways to market that widget. Instead, prove you know your stuff by including supporting data on why TV spots would work by, for example, pointing to successes with the same efforts in related categories or by competitors. Explain the reason you've selected the audience target using statistics on the preferences and spending power of the demographic. And, to really stand out, tie it all together with a few sketches (don't worry, we're not all artists; stick figures are a-okay) and a cost-benefit analysis of spending on development and purchase of ad spots and potential sales and profits. Quality rules over quantity.

Once you've established that your work is good—that

maybe you're even a bit indispensable (you'll know when you overhear comments like "What are we going to do when she goes back to school?" or "What do you mean, he leaves in less than a month?")—you can dip your toe into the other kind of above and beyond. Your mission: seek out opportunities to learn outside the assignments you're given. This can take several forms. You could volunteer to help with a project that interests you within your group or even with another team (but be sure to observe the cultural pluses and minuses of making such a request; if teams largely operate independently or even with a bit of competition among one another, it's probably not a good idea to ask to work with the "enemy").

You can also ask to sit in on department meetings or act as a fly on the wall in critical corporate meetings (just be sure to sit in a seat on the perimeter, unless invited to sit closer; the cushy leather chairs or pricey Aerons at the table are meant for participants and sitting closer could appear presumptuous). Another idea: if a fellow intern or a junior staffer is attending a seminar you think you could learn from, ask to go along. Don't be afraid to ask for opportunities to get involved with projects or work that will contribute to your professional development and benefit the company; just make sure to do it in a way that's within the norms of the company and your group.

MEETING PEOPLE OUTSIDE YOUR ZONE

Networking, plain and simple, is perhaps one of the most critical skills you'll need to build your career. A strong network will open doors for you every step of the way—from your first job to your fifth. Still, many people tend to shirk from networking during their college years because in the two-way street of professional connections, the less you know, the less you have to offer in return. Don't be like those people. Begin to build your network now, knowing that what you have to offer is enthusiasm and a willingness to learn—and a referral bonus.

Of course, this isn't a reason for someone to add you to their professional network, but it is something you have to offer as a newbie that you can keep in mind in those moments when you're not quite sure of yourself in reaching out. And in case you're wondering, most companies offer referral bonuses to employees who recommend job candidates who end up being hired. Some companies offer upward of $2,000 or more for even lower-level referrals. If you impress a new contact as someone who could be a strong addition to his company, he'll remember you when it's time to offer *his* boss input on potential candidates to interview for an opening.

Your internship is one of the first opportunities you have to build your professional network. Most of that will be done within the group you work with, but you'd be wise to branch out. As an intern, you're likely to have the opportunity to meet people you'd never meet otherwise. Many companies offer brownbag lunches or presentations that are open to all interns, even if the group they work with won't directly benefit for the session. Those are great places to meet people who work in other parts of the company (and then put on your networking hat). Even if those opportunities don't exist, you can still make connections. First, check with the internship supervisor or your boss to find out the most appropriate way to reach out to, say, a vice president in another department or your boss's counterpart who is in charge of a different set of projects down the hall.

THE ART OF NETWORKING AND STAYING IN TOUCH

Let's face it, for some people networking doesn't come naturally. And it almost never feels comfortable in the beginning, even for those who find it easy to talk to just about anyone. The difference, of course, is that the chat you're about to have has a motive that others don't: professional advancement. But you're going to have to get over that, because it's critical to network during an internship (although you don't need to come on too strong; subtlety is important, too).

In reality, your network is going to expand naturally, simply because you're working alongside people who have already begun their careers in a field you're just beginning to pursue. And often you're working side-by-side with other interns who come from different schools, backgrounds, and educational achievements. Each of them has his or her own network of contacts. Supervisors, employees, fellow interns, everyone you meet through your internship, should be added to your contact database, says Lindsey Pollak, a career expert, in her 2007 book *Getting from College to Career.*[13]

You'll be chatting with your peers, higher-ups, and others throughout each workday, but the key to real networking is to also attend as many events after work and informal get-togethers as you can. Even if you're just meeting up with fellow interns, that's valuable. One of them could land a job at your dream company down the road, and maintaining contact with that one fellow intern could be the key to your landing a job there, too. What's more, you never know who might be in another intern's own network. Pollak's advice for lateral networking: ask what other careers, companies, internships, or opportunities your peers are considering or have pursued already. Doing this can also help you get over any stage fright you might feel about networking with people who are senior to you.

Focus on the *quality* of the people you meet, not the quantity. That's particularly true when you're meeting people outside your immediate workgroup. Two good contacts in other departments or one strong informational meeting with the head of college-graduate recruiting can be more valuable than meeting ten less-interested or less-connected people.

Scope out which higher-ups are known to offer advice and time to interns and young employees, and when you contact them, make sure you are polite and ask for a meeting that

SHOULD YOU ASK FOR A RECOMMENDATION LETTER?

When you're just starting out, references can be hard to come by. And former internship supervisors might oversee dozens of newbies per year and have trouble a year later recalling specifics of your great summer performance.

While a generic recommendation letter isn't as good as one that is personalized for a specific job and company, getting a recommendation letter to send to potential employers when you launch a full-time job hunt can be smart. You can—and should—ask for a more tailored letter or personal reference when you land interviews. But even then, the generic note will come in handy as a memory-jogging tool for your former supervisor.

To get a letter of recommendation, you can ask your supervisor if he feels comfortable writing a note about your performance and your strengths that you could send to potential employers. You could also ask a senior staffer who worked closely with you to do the same. If there are specifics you want them to highlight, send a follow-up e-mail briefly saying so (and in that note, make sure you give specifics about yourself, such as your major and the projects you worked on over the summer). Do not attempt to write the note for them or be so specific that your recommender doesn't see room for his own opinions and observations.

Once you've got the document, send a thank-you note!

takes up no more than twenty minutes of their time. When you do meet with them, it's inevitable that the person will ask what you've been up to all summer. Don't fumble on this one: briefly describe—with enthusiasm—what projects you've worked on and one or two results. Ending with something like "I've really learned so much and that's why I wanted to meet with you" as a way to lead into your conversation is smart. Next, make sure you know something about this person's work and have specific questions or concepts you'd like to discuss. You might ask a follow-up question about the presentation he gave last week or you might simply ask him to offer some insight into his group and how it's different from the one you're embedded with.

College senior Emily Noonan says she learned the importance of networking finesse by watching those around her at a business symposium at the University of North Carolina, where she studied business administration. Networking, Emily says, isn't just about being chatty. It "requires research and thoughtful execution, so as to not have an introduction resembling a bad pick-up line." Good networking, she says, is fairly easy to spot. "The signs are the exchanging of business cards, mutual laughter at a joke, or even [an employee] and an exchange student conversing in Mandarin." At the symposium, which brought together sixty executives and four hundred students for a case competition, career panels and executive speeches, Emily says this became more obvious. "I saw more clearly than ever that the division between my classmates who were networking and those who weren't closely resembles the division between the ones who have job offers and interviews and those who don't."

The takeaway: learning to network and add to your list of professional contacts can make the difference between landing a first job . . . and moving back in with Mom and Dad.[14]

So, just how do you go from these informal chats to making someone a true member of your professional network? Sure, you can send them an invite on LinkedIn—and you should. Or you can informally keep in touch—and you should do that, too. But before you do either, be straightforward: ask your new contact if you can keep in touch with them after the internship and perhaps check in from time to time. Whatever you do, don't wait until you need to ask for career advice or a referral to make contact. Maintain the relationship with regular contact.

E-mail everyone who agreed to keep in touch with you a quick note within a few weeks of heading back to school; at the longest, e-mail them before Thanksgiving break. Your note needn't be too formal. Simply thank them again for the insight, help with an assignment, or career tips—or whatever it might be that solidified your connection—and express thanks to them for allowing you to stay in touch. If you've come across an article or paper that you think might interest a contact, send it along with a note explaining why you're doing so.

In fact, that's a good way to maintain contact over the following months—and will keep you from simply e-mailing a person only when you need something. Networking runs both ways; eventually you might ask a contact for help, so be respectful of her time and offer your own "help" when it makes sense. Staying on the radar screen can help you land a job—at best—and at the least, can keep you in the know about goings-on at a company or in the field.

KEEP INTERNING . . . EVEN AFTER SUMMER ENDS

Here's a little secret that many of your classmates might not know: a growing number of companies are locating satellite offices or divisional offices near the universities they like to hire new grads from so they can better tap into those talent pools. For example, Google, Campbell Soup Co., and Aeronova Aerospace—among others—all opened offices near University of Michigan in the last several years. Google and others have opened offices near Carnegie Mellon University for the same reason.[15]

What does that mean for you? For starters, if you've interned for a firm that has an outpost near your college or university, there could be a good chance you could keep working for the company part-time during the school year, either for pay or for credit. As your summer internship draws to a close, you can suggest to your intern supervisor or direct boss that you continue to work a few hours a week from the local office.

If you've established a strong track record and good rapport, this will be an easy ask, especially if there's work still to be done on projects you pitched in on.

No local office close by? If you've interned for a company in the same field or that has similar business lines to a company that does have an office near campus, you could parlay that experience into an off-season internship. It will take more legwork on your part, but if you have the right connections and come with good references, and since students who pitch themselves during the school year face less competition for coveted slots and many firms have just waved good-bye to their summer interns, you'll have a decent shot.

Another growing source of internships, often for credit—but all the same, the experience is what counts—stems from master research agreements that many schools are signing with large corporations. Penn State, for example, has about fifty such agreements with companies including DuPont and Lockheed Martin. Engineering powerhouse Purdue University has a similar number with companies such as Rolls-Royce Aircraft Engines and IBC Advanced Alloys (for a nuclear fuel effort).[16]

Even elite universities have gotten in on the game. Harvard College has an agreement with firms including Charles River Ventures and Polaris Venture Partners among its more than two dozen venture capital firm agreements, in addition to the other industries it partners with. Stanford University has master research agreements with companies including Amgen, Genentech, Hewlett-Packard, and Agilent, among others in the tech and biotech industries.

A quick Google search or school intranet search for master research agreements and your university's name will almost always lead to a Web page devoted to details on who your school has relationships with. In many cases these agreements primarily match professors and graduate students with big companies—either for research or consulting-like projects. But, increasingly, they're also paving the way for school-year internships, part-time work, and more. Figure out which professors in your major or interest areas are doing active research with the firms your school partners with and ask about assisting. Or if you have, say, taken a class with that professor or have developed a relationship, you could even ask for an introduction to someone in the firm who might be able to find—or create—an internship for you. In other cases, companies themselves initiate the student-intern relationships. At Purdue, for example, a professor's relationship with Rolls-Royce led to a group of undergraduate students working to improve some of the company's software to make the design process and the overall life cycle of Rolls-Royce aircraft engine parts more efficient.[17] Another bonus: the work you'll be doing will likely be leading-edge, say school administrators, providing you with valuable experience while also giving your résumé a boost.

WHEN YOUR INTERNSHIP
REVEALS A BAD FIT

Oh boy. It's not a pleasant moment—even if you saw it coming. Your internship went well. You walked away with praise and tangible results to show for your ten weeks of work. You feel fairly certain that an entry-level job at the company could be yours if you wanted it. But something just isn't right. You always dreamed of working in consulting—perfect for your analytical mind and your problem-solving, can-do people personality. But Big Consulting's corporate culture, constant travel, and seventy-hour workweeks look a lot less appealing after the last few months. Now what?

First, don't panic. Realizing that a certain type of job or corporate atmosphere is not right for you is actually a good thing. Why? Because knowing what you don't want in a career or a job brings you a step closer to figuring out what you *do* want. Perhaps working long hours for a huge brand-name firm isn't for you but consulting still appeals to you. In that case, you've got a stellar name on your résumé and can use that when you apply for jobs at smaller firms with a different culture.

If you find that the career itself is just all wrong, don't stress. Your efforts weren't all for nothing. Remember, you still have that entry on your résumé, not to mention the connections you made and the skills you learned. So where to go from there? Once you figure out what it was about the internship that you *don't* want in your future job, make a list of the things you did like about it, as well as the skills you took away that you most want to build on. Then figure out which industries and types of jobs rely on those skills and traits and set your sights on taking courses to round out your knowledge, educating yourself on the field(s), and looking for a way to get some sort of experience in the job (check out those master research agreements or local firms you could offer your services to for free or for credit . . . or perhaps even for pay). Better to discover this bad fit now than when you are five years into a career that makes you unhappy.

CHAPTER 3

LANDING YOUR FIRST JOB

Internships may be more crucial than ever for establishing your career track and pouring the foundation for your professional life, but the work you do in your first full-time job will be the true launching pad—the cornerstone, so to speak—of your professional career. A couple of strong internship experiences will make your résumé shine and position you to land that crucial first job. But what you did as an intern won't matter if you can't translate that—and all you've learned between those summer stints—into the day-to-day hum and demands of a position with responsibilities that don't end next month or next week, but rather build on one another to create the sort of experience that successful careers are built on.

But first, you've got to *land* that elusive first job. On many college campuses, there's a big push to start the job hunt early—sometimes as early as the minute you step foot back on campus in September of your senior year. For some fields that's entirely appropriate. Big banking and consulting and accounting firms, for example, often complete their new-grad recruiting four to six months before graduation; they've got a steady flow of promotions or experienced hires leaving for grad school that they can anticipate a year or more in advance. NACE's *2010 Student Survey* found that nearly 25 percent of 2010 graduates (surveyed two to four months before graduation) who applied for a job actually had one waiting for them after graduation (that's up from just under 20 percent in 2009). The majors most likely to receive an offer, according to the survey, are Accounting, 46.9 percent; Business Administration, 45.4 percent; Computer Science, 44.1 percent; Engineering, 41.0 percent; Social Sciences, 40.5 percent. But in other fields, many companies—even big names—are also delaying some hiring until much closer to or even after graduation. That just-in-time hiring isn't just a reflection of lingering economic uncertainty. Many companies say that this concept born out of the latest recession has proven to be so successful that they plan to continue it, even in flush times.

What this means is that if you are entering a field other than banking or finance, spring is an equally good time as the fall to land a good professional job. By spring, any midterm planning for the next several years is likely solidified and a company knows exactly what it needs and what kind of hires it needs to make in order to push forward for the remainder of the year and the few years ahead. Plus, with many companies pushing performance evaluations, raises, and bonuses to the early spring, firms often see a wave of promotions or job changes then that can impact hiring all the way down the ladder. Waiting, it turns out, can sometimes make for a better first-job experience for you, too, since often you won't simply be hired into a "class" of newbies but for a specific role or group of roles that is in demand at the time.

Landing that first job that's right for you professionally and personally will take time and effort, especially in a tough economy. Sure, there will be some things you can't control about your first job (like your title or your benefits) and some things you can control (the caliber of work that comes your way, the kind of environment and company you work for), but either way, welcome to the new first-job reality: the onus is on you to make your way into the right job. So whether you decide to start your search in September of your senior year or opt to wait until spring, from that day forward you should carve out time every week—perhaps even daily—for research and outreach and treat your job hunt as you would a class with deadlines, papers to write, and tests to study for.

And read on for just what you need to do to parlay your ambition, internship experience, education, and perseverance into a crucial first job on the professional career ladder.

PARLAYING THAT INTERNSHIP INTO A REAL JOB

If you were one of the lucky interns at a company that loves to hire back their trainees for full-time jobs after graduation, you've already got a leg up on the competition. But even so, you can't sit back and wait for the company to come to you with an offer. True some firms (most often accounting firms, some investment banks, and some consultancies) will make offers to their best interns before they return to campus (more on how to weigh whether to accept or keep looking in a bit), but most applicants will still need to go through the interview process, even for a position at a firm they've interned with.

If you've followed our advice so far, you'll be ahead of the competition. You did write those follow-up notes to all your new contacts from your internship, right? And you made sure to sit down for an informational interview session with HR or the most appropriate hiring managers before you left for the summer, right? Okay, good. Now you need to decide whether you liked the company you interned with well enough to truly want to work there full-time. After all, no sense in applying for a job that isn't going to be a good fit. Go back to that cultural observation you made. Does the environment bring out the best in you? Did you feel like you mostly fit in? And how about the work—was it challenging and exciting? Did it keep you interested and engaged (grunt work aside)? Is it an office atmosphere and a type of company that you could see yourself going back to day after day for a year or two? Will you be able to contribute and also learn something significant along the way to take to your next job? Does the company have a reputation for developing young staffers? Did the young employees you met or observed there seem happy?

If you find yourself nodding your head as you read these questions, that's a good sign that your summer employer could be a good full-time employer.

Now all you have to do is convince them of that. So what to do next?

If you've kept in touch with your supervisor or other staffers at the company, the first thing is to send a pleasant note updating them on your status as a soon-to-be graduate and on your continued interest in working at the firm (if you're graduating with some awards or at the top of your class, it doesn't hurt to mention that). The note could be as simple as, "Dear so-and-so, It's been several months since summer ended, but I continue to be very interested in pursuing full-time work at Big Widget. I saw that the proposal created by the team I worked with was a hit with the client. It's exciting to know I was part of that effort. By the way, to beef up my quant skills, I enrolled in advanced statistics and I think these skills will enhance my contributions to proposals and projects in the field in the future. I notice Big Widget recruiters will be on campus in a few weeks and I plan to attend the presentation. I'd be grateful for the chance to chat briefly about any entry-level positions you expect to fill in the spring or summer—or any advice you might have about meeting with the recruiting team. Thanks again for such a rewarding summer experience. Sincerely, John Q. Intern."

The key is to express your continued interest, and show that you've not only kept up with the goings-on at the firm but that you have been boosting your skills to be an even better fit for the company in the future. If it's closer to graduation, you should also peruse the company's online career portal for entry-level jobs that interest you and ask specifically to chat about those spots—or others—that will be filled soon.

One thing worth noting: don't flat out ask for a job. No-body wants to be put in the awkward position of being forced to field the "will you hire me" question. Hiring is often more complex and involved than just a hiring manager's desire to bring you aboard—even if he wants to. Creating that long pause in the conversation could make future conversations awkward. Instead, you should make your interest clear, and hope that your summer supervisor responds encouragingly—ideally by telling you how perfect you'd be for a slot coming open in a few months. In that case, your most important question: How do I apply?

WHEN YOUR INTERNSHIP DOESN'T LEAD DIRECTLY TO A REAL JOB

What if you had a good internship experience at a big Mid-western company, but know that you'd much rather live on the East Coast or be closer to family in the Southwest? Does that make your internship success all for nothing? Not at all. For starters, if the company has offices or subsidiaries in these alternate locations, you can use virtually the same contact strategies to keep your foot in the door. In some cases, new hires often prefer to work in a company's headquarters, mak-ing outpost spots tougher to fill. Your interest in them could help you stand out. Just be sure that the satellite offices and positions offer as high caliber an experience—or close to it—as you'd get at the home-base location. And know that it's possible you'll need to live in a less desirable location for a year or two in order to move to your ideal city. It's okay to ask about career paths that lead to another office.

These conversations are trickier if you left your internship with a passion for the industry but not for the company you worked with. Tricky doesn't mean impossible, however. You can still ask for a reference, a bit of guidance, or a push in the right direction from the people you met over the summer. You'll just need a little extra tact and savvy. If you've received a promise of a reference from a supervisor, that's a good place to start. Your note, in this case, might say something like this: "My internship last summer really helped me solidify my skills and get a better handle on what I want to do in the industry. I really want to move toward business development—something that Big Widget doesn't have a natural track to for new grads. That's why I'm targeting companies like Big Circle and Big Square, which have rotational programs that include business development for high-potential new grads. You mentioned before I left that I shouldn't hesitate to contact you if I needed career guidance or a good reference. Can I ask for a little of both? Do you have fifteen or twenty minutes in the next few weeks to chat by phone? I'd be grateful for some time to pick your brain about Big Circle and Big Square and maybe a few ideas about the best way to make inroads at those firms." There, that wasn't too hard.

With either approach, use that phone call to feel out your prospects and best bets for proceeding. Be polite, on time, and inquisitive. If you really want to work at the company, ask how other projects or assignments you worked on are going and inquire about whether or not the department or a related one might be adding staff. Inquire about whether there's a specific HR specialist or hiring manager you should be sure to get in front of. Remember, you aren't asking for a job, but rather, guidance on the best ways to get your foot in the door. If the company is coming to your campus soon, find out which representatives will be there and ask your contact if he knows these people. If he does, he might offer to mention your name or be able to give you some insight into the rep's preferences for being approached at school events or in first-round interviews.

If your call is one seeking advice about or connections to opportunities at other companies, you'll need to do a little extra homework before you pick up the phone. First, find out whether your contact has worked at those firms—or if he's hired staffers from the firm. Corporate bios are a good place to start. You can also quiz junior staffers you've kept in touch with to get some background information. Once you're armed with research, ask your former supervisor or contact to first share his thoughts about the companies and their entry-level positions and potential for growth. You might mention that you know your summer manager once worked at Big Square—ask why he left and whether he'd recommend any particular department (or conversely, advise you to steer clear).

Often the conversation will naturally lead to an offer to connect you with someone at the other firm. Bingo! You've just added someone new to your network. In hyper-competitive fields like investment banking, high-level strategy consulting, and sometimes technology, you're less likely to receive an offer to connect you to a competing firm, so don't push too hard. You're better off asking a fellow former intern or a junior staffer you got on well with over the summer about the competition. If the conversation doesn't lead to an offer to make a connection, be sure to ask the best way to get a reference before you hang up. And leave your chat open-ended by, say, asking if it's okay to e-mail if you have more questions.

Using Corporate Career Portals

These contacts are critical and—if you left a good impression—could be a key way to land an entry-level job. But these days there are ways to get information and leads on job openings even if you don't have a personal contact at a company. That's because companies who want to keep their brands fresh in the eyes of young talent have gone to great lengths—and big expense—to enhance their corporate career websites with everything from employee testimonials to detailed day-in-the-life stories to slideshows, videos, podcasts, and more on the various jobs and opportunities for advancement. In fact, as one article recently reported, at many big firms, job postings and plain-vanilla descriptions of corporate culture "have been supplemented with YouTube videos and blogs from employees, human-resource officials and even executives, along with links to corporate Flickr, Facebook, and Twitter pages that chronicle life at the company and include job postings."[18]

These efforts to attract young professionals like you mean you'll be able to get more information and insight than ever before about a company, its jobs, your potential for advancement, and more.

In a 2010 survey of 2,457 college students and recent graduates, Potentialpark found that the best career sites "go beyond information, and offer inspiration," appealing to "the emotional decision centers of their visitors."[19] Does this make you suspicious? That's generally a good instinct. There's bound to be plenty of propaganda in the testimonials and video blogs created by company employees, and therefore you should seek out other sources of information about working at the company. But they can still serve as a source of information—as long as you don't treat them like gospel.

Bottom line: poke around, take the testimonials with a grain of salt, but take advantage of the vast stores of information these sites provide. It wasn't all that long ago that you'd be hard-pressed to find much of anything useful about a company on its careers site.

USING PROFESSIONAL ASSOCIATIONS

Let's say you joined the American Advertising Federation (AAF) back in your sophomore year. You even attended a few symposiums and a career fair for students at a local chapter. And last year, you went to that networking event for young professionals. Can this help you in your search for a full-time job? With a little legwork, the answer is yes. Professional industry associations—and there are several hundred of them, spanning a huge range of fields and industries—really can serve as a useful networking tool.

Some may even serve up a dream job. The largest and

INDEPENDENT SOURCES OF INFORMATION ON WORKING AT A COMPANY

To supplement (or verify the accuracy of) any information you get on a company's own website, there are a number of third-party sites you can go to for more objective information about different employers or companies. These include the following:

WSJ.com/Careers: *The Wall Street Journal*'s career website offers a myriad of advice, insight, and career guides for jobseekers. Its "How I Got Here" and "PayGrade" stories, in particular, offer a glimpse at what it takes to build a career in specific industries or specific jobs.

FINS.com: A jobs-and-careers website from Dow Jones that serves as both a job board and an advice site offering Q&As on what it's like to work in various industries and companies, news on job openings in various sectors and companies, and more. The site currently features information on careers in finance and accounting; sales and marketing; and technology.

GlassDoor.com: A newer entrant into the market, this website offers anonymous reviews, salary information, and insights into what it's like to work at a multitude of companies from entry level to upper management. To get detailed reports, you have to sign up, but it's worth it just to get a look at one feature on this site: examples of interview questions recent applicants and new staffers say they faced.

CareerLeak.com: Focuses on entry-level and some midlevel jobs and includes reviews (listed by company) submitted by employees or ex-employees of the company. The quality of the information depends on what anonymous users provide, so details can be spotty. The site itself offers overviews of what it's like to work at the various companies and the most commonly listed openings and their requirements. One note: many of the companies and positions listed are not in professional fields or job categories, but the site is worth a look for the occasional entry-level professional job.

JobsInPods.com: This website allows companies to create podcasts about their job postings. It's not quite independent since the material is submitted by the companies, but the podcasts tend to be informative, detailed, and directed at specific groups or target audiences, such as women or diversity candidates.

Jobs.AOL.com: This semi-generic jobs and career website offers "what it's like to work at" features written by employees and former employees. Because they are outside the control of the companies featured, the insights are likely to present a fuller and more objective picture of a workplace and company than what you'd get on that company's site. Look under company research in the "Success Stories" category to get started. A "New Grads" section offers bits of useful insight into different fields and cultural norms at work.

most active, like the AAF, host career fairs across the country and maintain extensive job boards. Many also have college chapters that cater to burgeoning professionals in the field (hint: join now if you haven't already; just like networking, you don't want to join only when you need something). In some cases, for smaller companies or big firms who've whittled their list of on-campus treks, associations and their career portals or job fairs have replaced campus visits.

What's more, many associations sponsor student competitions or symposiums that can serve as opportunities to showcase your talents and also meet potential employers. It's not uncommon for hiring managers to mine such contests and symposiums for potential candidates. If you're looking for a job at a midsize company or a one-of-a-kind slot that you're not finding during on-campus recruiting, associations can also be a great resource for finding them in one place. And your willingness to pay the membership fee (discounted, of course, for students) is a strong sign that you're dedicated to the industry, which can give you a little leg up on the other candidates.

THE ON-CAMPUS INTERVIEW

It's still true that—unless you've secured a job from your summer internship already—at least half of your first interviews will come through your college or university career services office. And research shows that students who use the services of their college career services office are more likely to find jobs before graduation. That's partly because you'll find oodles of resources (from résumé help to mock-interview sessions to detailed research on companies and alumni databases) and you'll find a built-in system for applying to and interviewing for popular (and competitive) entry-level professional jobs.

While it's true that due to thinner staffs, fewer recruiters are coming to campus these days and that would-be employees are pushed to online career portals, many large firms still visit campus and expect to meet with interested students both at company presentations and in individual first-round interviews. If the firms you are interested in don't visit campus, the career center is still a good first stop to research those companies and find out if the school or its alumni have any contact information or an inside track to hiring at the company. Even if you're interviewing with the same company where you interned in a prior summer, you should approach an on-campus interview as your gateway to your first employer.

The fact that companies have drastically narrowed the number of schools they visit to recruit new grads means each slot they fill this way is more competitive than it was a few years ago. That also means that the interview will count more, and could be more intense or more focused than it was in the past. Luckily, with some preparation and practice, you can learn how to ace the first-job interview process.

THE FIRST INTERVIEW

Some people are just naturals when it comes to interviewing—don't worry if you aren't one of those people. You can become one (or fake it pretty well with practice). It's true that the interview is critical for assessing your skills and fit with the company and the job you're being considered for. But for soon-to-be grads building the foundation for their professional career, the key to a successful interview is in the presentation. You'll want to make a strong impression by appearing confident (but not full of yourself)—that is, prepared, well informed, and clear-spoken.

Many young professionals think acing an interview means getting the "right" answer to every question. This isn't really true. You can be a little off-target on a question or two and still be asked back for a second interview, as long as you hit the right notes at the core and show enthusiasm and key bits of knowledge. To do that, you need to prepare—and not like you do when cramming for an exam. The sort of preparation needed to stand out in an interview will take some extra effort on your part. Treat your preparation like a term paper or class project and set aside time for it on your calendar.

The first thing you need to know about interviewing for your first job: it will be quite different from the interview that landed you your internship.

The level of expertise that will be expected when you meet with recruiters is much higher. They'll ask the usual questions about fit and strengths and weaknesses—and there are plenty of great resources out there to help you answer those tricky interview questions. But remember, the stakes are much higher for the company now; they've got to decide on whom to spend thousands of dollars to fly to headquarters for another round of interviews with managers and execs whose time is valuable and limited. So after the formalities, expect to be quizzed on the technical aspects of the field and be prepared to apply what you know from class and your internships.

FRAMEWORK FOR ANSWERING COMMON QUESTIONS

Give me an example of a difficult situation you faced and how you handled it.

How to answer: The interviewer wants to see how you think and how you deal with other people and unexpected problems. Practice this one—at least a little—ahead of time and be sure to have a situation in mind that is easily relatable to the company and to the type of work you're seeking. Quickly explain the difficult situation (do not go on and on with details about all the factors involved), why it was a challenge, and how you pushed through and moved forward. As a kicker, explain what you learned and how you used that lesson the next time you got into a tough spot.

What are your biggest weaknesses?

How to answer: Keep it professional and be honest—but not too out there. Try to pick the most palatable weakness you have, say, saying yes to more work than you can actually handle, and then flip it around, "which means I end up working more than I should." But don't be disingenuous. If possible, you should also indicate how you are working on your weakness. If public speaking is a weakness, you might say "I still have some trouble speaking in front of large groups, but I've been practicing and actually made a presentation to a fifteen-person team last summer. Afterward, I asked my boss and a senior staffer for advice on what I could do better and I've really taken it to heart."

Tell me about yourself. . . .

How to answer: Do not take this question literally and deliver a litany of little-known facts about yourself (like the highlights of your wrestling trophies or the fact that you love dogs, but just the ones you can fit in a purse). Instead, discuss some of your strengths and professional interests; the things you say will set the framework for further questions, so focus on your skills, motivations, and professional desires.

Why do you want to work here?

How to answer: This is a biggie. Do your homework on the company and carefully explain how your skills, training, and personality fit into the goals and culture of the firm. Show you know your stuff with stats and information about the company and the industry. Just don't overdo it.

Why should we hire you instead of someone else?

How to answer: This is your chance to sell yourself. Reiterate why you are a good fit for the job and why you believe you will be able to make a big contribution to the company, its bottom line, its business, etc. Substantiate your answers with quick examples or by drawing on answers you've given in the interview that you are sure impressed the interviewer.

Where do you see yourself in five years?

How to answer: The interviewer wants to see how well you assess short-term goals and how clearly you understand what it might take to reach them. Rather than say you want to hold X position in five years, walk through it. You might say, "In two years, I'd hope to move from account assistant to junior account manager and within five years, I want to be in a full-fledged account management role, handling my own clients from start to finish." You might also be slightly more vague and say that titles are less important to you than moving on to more challenging roles with bigger responsibility—that you are open to opportunities as long as you are growing and contributing.

Do you have any questions for me?

How to answer: At the very least, ask about next steps and ask if there are any materials you can offer up to help support your candidacy. It's likely most of your questions will have been answered during the interview, but if not, make sure your questions are smart and pointed, directly related to the job of the next steps in the interview process.

Here are five key steps you should take to prepare for and ace your first-round job interview:

1. RESEARCH, RESEARCH, RESEARCH.

You'd be shocked to hear that a vast majority of otherwise smart, upward-trekking young people don't bother to do enough homework to be able to discuss basic aspects of a company's business or why they'd fit in at the firm. It seems like a no-brainer, of course. But then you get busy with exams or that term paper you really want to ace and suddenly the interview day is upon you and you haven't done any research. Take note: no matter what else you have going on, DO NOT skimp on your company research. It can make or break your candidacy and it's impossible to fake having done it (in fact, doing so makes you look worse in most cases). Here's what you need to know: the company's key products, businesses, and clients; key competitors; latest industry news and goings-on (you can set up a Google alert to receive news and press releases on the firm and the industry to stay up to date in the weeks leading up to the interview); and areas of growth—especially if they're related to the job you're vying for.

To find all of this, start with the company's website and look to databases like Hoovers.com or even at SEC filings. You can also peruse local newspapers and monitor industry association websites for big issues facing the industry. Google the person you'll be interviewing with, too. You might find some commonalities that you can tap into during the interview.
If you have your heart set on working at a particular company, you can deepen your research by contacting alumni who've landed a similar job at the company in the last year or so and ask about what skills they're most using, what traits are most valued in new hires, and the like. Ask for any tips on interviewing, too. And check out interview tips the company itself offers on its website or career center material. Once

you've got all this research in hand, match your skills, experiences, and strengths to what you've learned and be prepared to apply them to interview questions you'll be asked.

2. PRACTICE.

Chances are, you've already had a few successful interviews. After all, you've landed two good internships already, right? So the idea of practicing for an interview with someone whose style you don't know and whose questions might be hard to anticipate might sound like a waste of time. But, it isn't. It's nearly a guarantee that you'll be asked some form of several basic interview questions, including these: Why do you want to work at this company? What are your biggest strengths and weaknesses? Where do you see yourself in five years? Can you tell me a little about yourself? Quick, try to answer one of these right now. Not so easy to pull off the top of your head. Granted, you don't want to sound like you've rehearsed a boring monologue word for word, but you do want to be prepared. And that's where practicing comes in.

For some people, it can be as simple as jotting down a few notes and repeating them aloud—almost as you would for a class presentation. For others, actually role playing an interview can be useful (peer advisors at the career center are a good place to start; otherwise, grab a friend who is also interviewing and quiz each other by randomly asking common interview questions). The key is to get comfortable enough with the framework of your answer—but not to have a completely scripted answer in your pocket, ready to whip out before the question even leaves an interviewer's mouth.

Also important: know your résumé. Seems obvious, but it may have been months since you updated or looked at it, and you'll come across looking foolish if you forget even the smallest detail. Before you go into an interview, review the document to remind yourself of dates you were employed, the tasks and responsibilities you listed, and anything else an interviewer might hone in on. That service award you won freshman year might just come up, so refresh your memory on the specifics.

3. KNOW WHAT YOU KNOW—AND HOW TO DEAL WITH THE REST.

Let's face it, you're just twenty-one or twenty-two years old. Nobody expects you to know the same things someone with five years on a job would know. But you will be expected to have the ability to apply the experiences and skills you've gained in prior internships to the job you're interviewing for, starting with the interview.

So, how do you figure out what you know? Take out a pencil and paper, or slide over to the computer. You've done your research on the company, its industry, and the job or job type you're interviewing for, maybe even contacted a recent hire at the firm for more detailed information, so you know what the job might require. Jot those down in one column. Next to that, write down the knowledge and skills you have that match—and why. For example, in the first column, you might write, "quick thinking and decision making." And next to it, you'll detail an example from your prior internship or work experience with something like "When I worked with the analysis group at Big Widget, I had less than an hour to think through two proposed ways of defining a key set of data we were going to use. I quickly hashed out the pros and cons of each and came to the conclusion that we were better off using one over the other because, even though the second way could get us what we needed, the first option would be easier to apply directly to the rest of the project and save steps later." Refreshing your memory with such examples will be invaluable when the interview questions begin.

When you get to a skill or trait that you don't have an example for, don't try to fake it. Instead, write a sentence about how you might try to gain that skill or trait. Imagine an interviewer asking you about your knowledge of a particular software program that you've never once used. Stammering over an answer or trying to pretend as if you know what you're talking about when you don't is far worse than recalling that answer you prepared in advance that said, "I'm not as familiar with that program as I am similar ones like X and Y, but I'm a fast study and I'm sure I can pick it up quickly. I learned program X in just a day or two and was teaching it to other interns by my second week at Big Widget." The key here is to be prepared for a range of questions on what you know, how you can apply your knowledge, and how you'll grow in areas where you're not yet competent.

If you stumble on a question that you haven't prepared an answer for, politely say that you're not familiar with that concept or skill but would be very eager to learn. There's no shame in admitting you don't know something, so long as it's not expected that you should know.

4. MIND YOUR MANNERS.

Dress professionally. In most cases, a suit is in order. Show up a few minutes early so you can get comfortable in the office— but not *too* early. Hiring managers' biggest pet peeves include candidates who show up more than ten minutes early; if you arrive earlier than that, wait nearby before you go in. Remember, interviewers are busy, perhaps with other candidates or with their daily work. Knowing you're out there pacing the lobby or interview room waiting area is disconcerting. You don't want *that* to be your first impression.

When you meet the interviewer, firmly shake hands, say hello, and thank her for meeting with you. Let her lead the initial small talk and be friendly but professional (hint: unless you're interviewing for a job as a party planner, don't mention the over-the-top party you went to if you're asked how your weekend was). Never interrupt when you're being asked a question. When you answer questions, focus on your tangible accomplishments and don't rush through complex answers. Watch closely for cues that your answer is off-track or getting too long; if an interviewer's attention seems to wander or his or her facial expression becomes blank, that's a sign you should wrap up your answer and move on.

5. WRAP UP STRONGLY.

Plenty of people breeze through the bulk of an interview with confidence and good answers, until they get to the end, when the interviewer asks if they have any questions about the company or the job. That's where things often get murky. Believe it or not, recruiters say a significant number of applicants get that deer-in-the-headlights look when asked if they have any questions or, worse, confidently proclaim they've don't have a single one. Neither is a good move. Come to the interview prepared with at least two questions about the company or the team you'd be working with if you were to be hired. These should be the kinds of questions that help you get a deeper understanding of the company or what it's like to work there—this isn't the time to ask about vacation time or benefits. Instead, ask questions about the typical track of an employee in the role you're seeking or about corporate culture. If the questions you came prepared with were largely answered during the interview, take a moment to think about something the interviewer brought up and ask a follow-up question. The idea is to both appear—and truly be—engaged and show that you are eager to learn something new that will help you decide whether you want to join the firm if you receive an offer.

Once you've worked through your questions, thank the interviewer for her consideration and her time. Ask if you can follow up should you have more questions about something specific you discussed. And before you get up, inquire about next steps and ask if there's anything else *you* can provide to help strengthen your candidacy. When you get back home, send a quick note thanking the interviewer for taking the time to meet with you—and for considering you for the job. Keep it simple.

WOWING THEM IN THE SECOND ROUND

You've made the cut and are moving on to round two. That means your hard work, preparation, and internship experiences—plus your performance in the first interview—have set you apart from at least some of the competition. In most cases, second-round interviews will be more intense and involve more people than a first-round interview. That means more preparation, and more research.

Once you get a schedule for your second round of interviews, if it's not clear who each person is in relation to the job you're vying for (i.e., Will he be your boss? Your bosses' boss? Your colleague?), ask the person who arranged the schedule. Knowing who, say, the direct supervisor is versus the higher up but indirectly involved executive can help you sort out whom you need to connect with most (while you do want to impress the higher-up, it's more important to form a bond with the person you'd report to day-to-day in the job).

Once you have a sense of who's who, find out about all the people you'll be meeting with. Corporate bios on the company website are one place to start. LinkedIn is another good source. Your goal should be to get a sense for each person's accomplishments, background, and, again, any commonalities you might have. Knowing that you grew up in the same town as your prospective boss or had a successful internship at the same company where he got his start can make for good small talk and help create a comfort level in conversation. Sharing a college alma mater is an even stronger bond—and you probably won't be the first to bring up that connection.

The key to acing a second-round interview is knowing what, exactly, the company is looking for. Second-round interviews are typically used to assess how ready you are to contribute to the firm. The interview questions are likely to be more technical and dig deeper into both your actual knowledge and your critical-thinking skills than the first-round interview, which may be more about getting to know you. Interviewers will be looking for how comfortable you are when you don't know the answer to a question, and judging your ability to learn the ways of the firm. They'll also be looking for clues as to how well you'll fit into the office culture and norms. And, almost like an umbrella over these things, they'll be looking for a big intangible: your potential to develop and move up at the company.

Go back to the recently hired alums at the company and ask them for insight about the people you'll be meeting with and the types of questions you might be asked. You should also delve deeper into what it takes to succeed in the job or type of job you're seeking. Go back to those third-party websites for clues from recent interviewees about the sort of questions that were thrown at them. Yours might be a bit different, but the concepts and line of questioning are likely to be similar within a group or division.

Once you've got some sense of what you might be asked, go back to that prep sheet you created for the first-round interview. Revise and add to it based on what you learned in the first interview and what you discovered in your subsequent research. Note any questions or types of questions your original interview focused on more than others and prepare deeper answers for those. If there were any technical or self-reflective questions that you stumbled over, brush up so you can answer these better if they're asked again or in a different way.

You're likely to be faced with either a series of interviews one after the other, a group interview, or several meetings in one day with a few people at a time. Depending on the field, you might be asked to take a skills test or work through hypothetical problems, projects, or cases. Ask up front what the second-round format will be.

One final note: if you've made it this far, you also want to

CASE INTERVIEWS: THE MOST FEARED OF ALL

In a case interview, you'll be given a business problem, situation, or challenge to consider and be asked to find a solution—fast. This type of interview is most used by consulting firms, but other companies use the tactic in less-intense ways. You'll be asked to analyze the situation, identify key business issues, and discuss how you would address them.

"Case interviews are designed to scrutinize the skills that are especially important in management consulting and related fields: quantitative skills, analytical skills, problem-solving ability, communications skills, creativity, flexibility, the ability to think quickly under pressure, listening skills, business acumen, keen insight, interpersonal skills, the ability to synthesize findings, professional demeanor, and powers of persuasion. Above all, the firm will be looking for someone who can do the real work at hand," says QuintCareers.com.

To ace the case, you'll need to do the following:

- Practice, practice, practice. Many consulting firms even have practice guides (like this one for Bain & Company, http://www.bain.com/bainweb/pdfs/acethecase.pdf) on their websites, and other career and consulting sites offer tips, too.[20]

- Be up on current business practices. Read business newspapers and periodicals that relate to the field so you get a sense of best practices and are well versed in how companies have solved their problems in the current business environment.

- Listen more than you talk—mostly. Listen carefully to the question and the setup of the problem. Take notes. Then keep quiet for a few minutes to gather your thoughts. It's expected and is a sign of maturity. After all, you wouldn't jump in with an answer to a multifaceted problem in two seconds on the job, right?

- Ask questions if you need clarification. These interviews are meant to provoke a back-and-forth. The person interviewing you will look for clues as to how you think and process challenges and incomplete information by listening to the questions you ask. And you can get clues about the most important information you need to solve the case. Just be sure your questions are clear and direct and don't make a barrage of inquiries; narrow down the information you need before you speak.

- Discuss. In addition to asking questions, remember that case interviews are meant to be two-way, almost discussion-like in nature. Engaging in the discussion is critical because how you engage and handle the back-and-forth and the information you receive will be part of how you are judged.

- Construct a framework to answer the question. Before you start to answer, jot down a short outline of the steps to solving the problem and prioritize what is most important, second most important, and so on. There's no one right answer, but logic, thought process, and critical thinking are key, so speak and answer clearly and explain why and how you reached your solution.

- Communicate clearly. McKinsey & Company's case interview tips sheet online recommends that you stay on one train of thought, but that "if you have considered some alternatives and rejected them, tell the interviewer what and why."[21]

use the second-round interview as an opportunity to make sure this company, and the position you're seeking, will be a good fit with your professional goals. Remember, this could be the company where you get your real professional start and you're evaluating the firm just as its executives and hiring managers are evaluating you.

WEIGHING YOUR OPPORTUNITIES: WHAT'S IMPORTANT

Everything you've read so far has been focused on the things you need to do to land your first job: measure your skills and interests, decide on the type of work that excites you, find and land a strong internship, study up on potential employers, and prepare yourself to wow interviewers. Now, the payoff: you've been offered a job. Perhaps you've secured offers from two employers.

The decision you make—whether to accept an offer—is about far more than the salary or title. To be sure, as a new grad, you've got less wiggle room for deciding on the little perks that you can negotiate when you're more experienced. But this job will be that first big building block for your professional life, and that means you should make some clear calculations about what's most important to you—and to your career—as you weigh job opportunities and offers.

Since this is your first job, you won't have a lot of leeway to negotiate salary and responsibilities (that's especially true at large companies, less so at small firms). But that doesn't mean you should necessarily just take the first offer that comes along. Finding a position that is right for you could mean that taking a job at a big brand-name company might not be the best move if it means relocating to a city you hate or if it involves heavy travel and you've got a fear of flying. Those are extremes (and some might say you can get over either of those issues). But if you have more than one offer or expect to, it's worth your time to analyze what the job itself— the actual work, mentorship, future opportunities, perks, work conditions, and more—offers you compared to others.

What variables exactly should you weigh? For your first job, the most important considerations go to the core of building your career. Here's what to ask yourself as you evaluate offers:

1. *How deep and broad is the work I'll be doing?*
    It's important to try to strike a balance. You don't want to be seen as too much of a specialist (unless, of course, you're in a cutting-edge field or a rapidly expanding area where in-depth knowledge of a specialty is sorely lacking) early in your career because it could mean being pigeon-

holed into the same sort of work for years to come. You also don't want the work you do to be so broad that you won't gain worthwhile knowledge and skills in much of anything. That will keep you from moving up (and out) because your value for another position will be hard to judge.

A job focused on a handful of core tasks and functions, with the possibility of exposure to other departments or teams through, say, joint projects or presentations, is often a happy medium. At the end of your first year, you want to be able to quickly explain two or three skills you've built and another two or three skills you're developing. For example, a junior business analyst might be able to say, "I've performed three strategic analyses in two different business functions in our company in the last year and presented two in-depth proposals to my group for consideration. I've also assisted creating a plan to implement one of the proposals and started to learn some of the technical requirements the proposal would entail."

To figure out what skills and expertise you will gain in the first twelve months, ask your potential boss or the recruiter making the offer to spell out what someone in the job is likely to learn and know by the end of their first year. You can also reach out to alumni who have been in a similar position with the company in the last three years—anyone further away from graduation might not have a strong sense of how the jobs are structured now.

2. *How much can I learn from my boss and more senior colleagues?*
You could be in the first job of your dreams, one with lots of potential and plenty of possible exposure to core functions of the firm—and it could still be a dud if your boss is unwilling or unable to teach you much of anything or if your colleagues are stingy with their knowledge. Now, there's a difference between having a boss or coworker

hold your hand through tasks and assignments you should largely be able to do on your own—that simply isn't going to happen, and if you need that, you'll have a hard time moving up and around in the future.

Working in a group where your boss and colleagues will help guide you through the trickier aspects of professional work—like the nuances of dealing with a client face-to-face gained from years of working with that client, or the secret to getting a proposal read faster by the boss gleaned from many personal attempts—will prove to be invaluable to your development.

For starters, these are signs that your boss or senior staffers will take an interest in your career and your success; a boss who is begrudging of his time or who doesn't advocate for talented young staffers is going to make for a tough first job—and more important, a difficult reference for later. And it's these implicit and unstated rules of office life and work performance that can trip up even the smartest and most appropriately ambitious young professionals. Granted, you likely won't find a workplace where every colleague or boss is generous, smart, and good to work with, but you also don't want to work with a group where most people are generally the opposite.

These things can be a bit hard to assess from afar, so it's best to reach out to recent grads who've worked for the same boss or with some of the same staffers. You can also check out a potential boss or colleague's LinkedIn profile to see if they know someone you know and take it from there. If you interned with the firm making the offer, but in a different department, check with career services to see if other students interned in the department or reach out to those interns you've kept in touch with from other universities (you didn't forget how important adding those folks to your network is, did you?) to see if they've got any insight themselves or if they have friends who interned in the department. And don't forget to ask what it's like to work for your would-be boss—and with your would-be colleagues. You'll work with these people day in and day out and they'll have an impact on your general happiness at the office—and on your success.

3. *Is this company committed to developing young recruits?*
A high percentage of new-grad hires leaving after a year or two is not a good sign. It usually means that the company doesn't provide many opportunities for advancement or that it's a difficult place to work for young professionals. Either way, unless the skills you'll gain at this company are a hot commodity in the job market or taking the job is critical to your hoped-for career path, it's probably best to steer clear. That's true even if you don't plan to stay in your first job for more than a year or two anyway. Why? People who leave so quickly are often unsatisfied or unchallenged, and that means the skills you might gain in those one to two years may not actually be all that great to begin with.

Conversely, a company with clear, lockstep development paths for young employees might not be a best bet, either. If the paths created are too rigid, it will be hard to take a different track if something tangential to your immediate work sparks your interest. If a company has a set training rotation, consider whether you'll get enough exposure to each function to figure out what fits you best— three or four months is usually a minimum for that.

Ask your would-be boss, the recruiter, or recent grads at the company what the company offers in the way of career development. The best will offer—and pay for— certifications you need, have set milestones while allowing for some flexibility and a broad range of training, and have a reputation for recognizing good work and promoting from within without too many extraneous restrictions on when, who, and how one can move up and around in the organization.

4. *Do I like the culture of the company and will it bring out the best in me?*

It can be difficult to decipher culture when you're not yet immersed in it. But you can use some of the same tactics you used in your previous internships—like doing your homework about the company—to get a feel for the overall atmosphere. When you speak to recent alums at the firm, ask about the culture. What's the work ethic like—is face time more important than getting a task done efficiently? Does the environment foster creativity and welcome ideas or is it more by the books? Are sharp elbows required to survive and thrive or do people work collaboratively?

If a company or department has a reputation for a certain kind of culture, take that reputation seriously because there's usually some truth behind it. Imagine yourself working there each day. Did you feel you could do your best work? Consider culture or nature of class projects, internship experiences, and other nonwork scenarios. In what kind of environment and culture did you shine—and, conversely, what environment left you at less than your best?

A me-first or sharp-elbowed culture is not going to be a good place to develop your critical first-job skills if you're the outgoing and collaborative type. Meanwhile, a culture where everyone goes to lunch together each day and throws joint birthday parties is going to make you uncomfortable if you're a private person who likes to leave work at the office. The key is to find the best fit for your personality (remember, perfect is elusive at any experience level)—one in which you feel fairly certain you'll be able to feel comfortable and excel.

You should also step back and ask yourself if the company philosophy is in line with your personal values, and whether it offers products, services, and business lines that you feel good about, believe in, and are interested in learning more about.

5. *How valuable will the skills I gain be when I look for my next job?*

For professional newbies, this can be difficult to assess, particularly since even the most career-certain among us can be lured down a different career path once exposed to all that's out there. For example, you might go into a job at an investment bank being absolutely sure you want to work in mergers and acquisitions but discover that what you really love is investment research—and not deal-making. So it's important for your first job to help you gain the solid foundation of skills for more than one possible next step.

Don't worry, most jobs—except for those that are highly specialized—will do that to some extent. But you should still be thinking about whether this job will allow you to develop some of the core skills that will help you land your *second* professional job—and be willing to walk away from an offer that won't provide some or most of them. Above all, you'll want to be sure your first job will help you sharpen your ability to think critically and work both independently and as part of a team, as these skills will be useful no matter what your next step.

Then look for positions in which you can build skills like analysis (of whatever subject or business you're working in), presentation skills (be it internal or to clients), and organizational know-how (be it through projects, teamwork, individual assignments, or just your own workspace and workflow) and have a chance to learn any software or techniques used widely in the industry. You should also look for jobs that will allow you to hone soft skills such as persuasion and professional communication. Finally, consider whether the job will offer more responsibility as you prove yourself.

In short, the smart professional is always thinking ahead. Remember, in a few years when you begin to look for your second job, you'll want to be able to give hiring managers specific examples of skills you've gained and mastered and be able to show successes and new responsibilities—be it projects that won clients over, participation in work that saved your company money or increased its revenue, or something else. If the job you're offered now won't allow you to do that in a few years, think twice before accepting.

6. *Is this really what I want to do every day?*
That sounds like a dumb question, I know. But here you are, staring a job offer in the face—finally! After you've evaluated the offer thoroughly, stop for a moment and ask yourself if you'll be excited to come to work most days, if the kind of work and the company you'll be doing it for will keep you motivated, engaged, and on your toes. No job is candy and flowers every day and there'll surely be days when you stare at the elevator in the lobby and wonder if you can really press the Up button. But there will be far fewer of those days—and they'll be easier to recover from—if you know that the work is what you want to do every day for the next year or two.

THE NEGOTIATION PROCESS

You're young. It's your first job. You're lucky to have been chosen from out of the pool of equally talented applicants. You should just take what you're offered, right? Not always. In fact, negotiating now might be your first opportunity to set your foot firmly on the fast track, and will set you up for better earnings in the future. In fact, a twenty-two-year-old who secures a $2,000 increase in annual salary at his or her first job will, because of the compounding effects of years of raises to follow, most likely generate roughly $150,000 in extra income over the course of a forty-year career, according to salary experts. Plus, though it can be difficult to tastefully and successfully negotiate, learning how to do it now will make it easier to ask for perks and raises—and a better package—at your next job, or the next time you're faced with the opportunity.

The worst that can happen: your would-be employer says no to your requests. As long as you negotiate respectfully and react gracefully to the company's response, you've strengthened your position, not weakened it. According to the Society of Human Resource Management, some 80 percent of employers are willing to negotiate salary. But hiring managers repeatedly say that very few people—some stats report less than one-third—actually do try to get a better starting salary. This is basically leaving money on the table. Try not to worry about whether negotiating or asking for something will make the company pull the offer. That rarely happens. What's more, the company has probably pored over thousands of applicants and decided you are among the best, you are someone it really wants to bring aboard. The others in the "B" file are just that—second-best choices. Plus, it will cost them time and money to go back to the drawing board. Point is, the firm is already invested in winning you over. Yes, even in a tough economy.

And remember, negotiations aren't just about salary. In some cases, entry-level salaries are fairly set. For example, rotational programs and cohort-oriented entry-level jobs at investment banks and the like can be fairly rigid. Everyone is paid the same—or close to it—with any differences based on location or, in some cases, your alma mater. But even in cases where the starting salary is not up for discussion, most of the time you can ask for more—such as perks, educational opportunities, start-date flexibility, vacation time, and wiggle room to pursue passion projects or charitable hobbies.

ROTATIONAL PROGRAMS: WHAT YOU NEED TO KNOW

For many new grads, a rotational program can be a great way to develop an all-around knowledge of a company and industry and work your way into a management role quickly. You'll rotate through—usually in three- to six-month periods—every important slice of a company, such as operations, sales, strategy, finance, business development, marketing, and more.

Originally these programs were used to train engineers to be managers. But they've proven so valuable that many large and midsize companies across industries have adopted them. While they won't give you a deep understanding of any one function, you will gain broad knowledge of many departments and businesses and quickly learn how they all work together to make the company successful. What's more, you'll gain all of this in about two years—a far shorter period of time than you'd be exposed to so much in a traditional entry-level slot.

To land a coveted spot in a rotational program, you'll need to demonstrate strong leadership skills. You'll also need to show that you know more than just the basics of the field—strong, in-depth internships and part-time work or a semester in a co-op program are often the kind of experience companies look for. Any research or accomplishments you can point to are a plus. Companies select candidates for these slots because they have the potential to run a group or department, and perhaps down the road, a division of the company or more.

If you end up in a rotational program, you can typically expect to be in a junior management or more-senior staff role in one of the departments (often the one you excel in and are most interested in) when you complete the rotations. You'll usually be classified as "high-potential" and continue to receive broad training in management and leadership.

Whether you're negotiating money or perks, the two most important things are (a) be prepared with information to back your requests and (b) know the *right way* to ask for what you want. Prepare by educating yourself on what other entry-level positions at similar firms are offering. Consult your peers and classmates and ask for any salary surveys your school's career services office might have conducted in the last year or two.

Look to outside expert websites, like Payscale.com, Glass Door.com, WetFeet.com, and others, to get a sense of the entry-level salaries for similar positions in your geographic area (compensation can vary a good deal depending on whether you're going to be working in, say, Minnesota, or New York City). It's critical to know the market value of the job, title, and function you're negotiating around. You should also seek out information on industry standards and best practices for other perks like vacation, education reimbursements, review-and-raise intervals, bonus opportunities, development opportunities, and the like. Remember, some perks will matter to you more than to other people (for example, while Joe thinks an on-site day care is a great perk, it's probably meaningless to you before you have children).

Now that you're armed with this knowledge and research, figure out what you want within the range of what's realistic. Start with salary, then write down your hoped-for bonus, vacation, educational opportunities, and other perks. Then lay out a plan for what you'll ask for in order of its importance to you. When you negotiate, start with the most important. Oh, and when you ask, do it by phone or in person (not e-mail). I know, I know, asking can be painful enough on its own, but it's best to address your requests in person or by phone. Practice with a friend or career services counselor to gain confidence if you need to.

Here are some tips how to ask the *right way.*

Salary. Before you get to the nitty-gritty of what to ask for, consider this: Is this your dream job? Or is this just a pretty great job—and you need a job, right? The answer will inform how you negotiate your first salary, says Ken Sundheim of KAS Placement.[22] He also suggests "in a roundabout and professional way, tell a potential employer that you want more money, but compensation is not a deal-breaker." You might say something like, "I've wanted to work for your firm since I began my job search and I'm excited about this offer. I've noticed that it's a bit lower than what some of my peers are being offered/what other comparable firms are offering and I wondered if there was any flexibility on starting salary?" If the hiring manager says no, accept the response gracefully and—after you ask for anything else you think you can negotiate—accept cheerfully and let the manager know you can't wait to start.

If the offer is a good one, but not a dream job or with your dream firm, you'll feel less nervous when you approach the negotiation and you can tone down the way you ask. You might say something like, "There are many things to like about this offer. I think this job will be a good fit. But I was aiming for a starting salary of XYZ, considering the typical starting pay in the industry and the fact that I've had two solid internships in the field at competitor firms already."

Either way, Sundheim writes, "Keep it short and sweet. Do not feel as if you have to explain yourself or go over your qualifications. The person sitting on the other side of the table understands them and this is why he or she is presenting you with an offer in the first place."

Bonus. If you get a no to your salary request or you receive a second offer that still falls short of what you think is a fair first salary, it's time to bring up incentive pay. If you've already been given a bonus target or range with your initial offer, ask if, in lieu of the extra pay, your bonus threshold could be raised.

You'll still have to prove yourself worthy of the bonus, of

course, but, you're (hopefully) planning to put in 110 percent anyway, especially if it's your first job. Plus, and if you earn that extra bonus, you'll have a better case for asking for a bigger raise or bonus floor later. You can also ask if your salary or bonus floor can be renegotiated after some period of time, say six months, based on your performance.

Reviews and raises. Along the same lines, you can—and should—ask for a review and the possibility for a raise after, say, six months. First, find out what the typical review and raise schedule is (it's usually one year) and ask for that to be accelerated, particularly if other compensation isn't negotiable. Asking for an accelerated review as part of an accelerated compensation request shows you're serious about proving your worth and is a low-risk way for the company to offer some rewards.

Vacation or start date. In some cases, free time or a flexible start date will be far more important to you than extra salary or bonus opportunities. If you know that up front, it's easy enough to tell the hiring manager that instead of seeking a higher salary or bigger bonus, you're asking for a start date that's a few weeks later than proposed, or an extra week of vacation.

If you are able to align your request with the goals or values of the company, that's all the better. For example, if the firm is known to support employees' charity work, you might say you'd like the extra week of paid vacation so you can stay involved in a nonprofit you've volunteered with for years. Some companies, like Ernst & Young, even allow staffers to take paid time off to do volunteer work, although that perk is usually limited to employees who have been with the firm for a certain period of time (often a year or more). If that's the case, ask that you be extended the same perk after six months instead.

Professional development. A big part of advancing your career might involve certifications or licensing. And many companies will help pay for the courses and exams needed to earn those. In some cases that perk will already be a part of the job offer. If not, ask for it. Use details and specifics if you can. For example, you might say, "To really excel in this role and eventually move up to the next one, it seems important to have XYZ certification. I notice that Big University offers a course for that beginning a few months after I'd join your company. Will I be able to apply for such a class and will the company pay for the course?" You should also ask about attending conferences and seminars in the field and, again, offer specifics about which ones and when you'd like to attend. (These will both benefit your first job skills and serve to build your professional network.)

This might be less a negotiation question and more a statement of what you want to get out of the job. Even if the answer is "It depends on how you're doing in the job," asking can demonstrate your commitment and desire to master the job and to advance.

CHAPTER 4

YOUR FIRST
YEAR AT WORK

The value you get from the first year on the job can be hard to measure. You'll still be learning the ropes, getting a grip on corporate culture, and figuring out how to impress the bosses. Slowly—and sometimes quickly—you'll begin to see how your contributions impact your team and your company. In that first year on the job, getting the little things right, understanding corporate culture (yes, you can change it some, but not your first week), and figuring out the extra career-boosters that will help you stand out, will be just as important in building your professional reputation and setting yourself up for a rewarding and solid career as your skill set and expertise. But this is going to require some patience, humility, and willingness to learn.

PAYING YOUR DUES

You're ready. You're eager. You're smart and capable. It's all the makings of a take-the-world-by-storm career. But don't make the same mistakes many ambitious careerists make by giving off a vibe that says you want to run the place in, oh, a year or two (or maybe now). Before you start gunning for the top, it's critical to watch, learn, and prove yourself in the tasks and projects you're assigned.

So listen up: forget the fact that you made the dean's list every semester or that you were at the helm of three clubs and graduated magna cum laude. Come your first day of work, none of that is going to matter all that much. Putting those achievements out of your mind isn't going to be easy; ambitious college seniors are often used to being in charge, be it as captain of a sports team, a student government representative, or the like. But you'll need to set that aside. At your new job, you are, well, the new kid. Sure, you're still bright and ambitious, but no matter what you achieved in college, the slate has been wiped clean, and it's now up to you to prove that you can be the same sort of leader and high achiever in the office. Start by being humble and taking stock of the performance and expectations of your boss and more experienced colleagues. First up is learning the often-unspoken-but-all-important rules of the office.

THE OFFICE RULES YOU NEED TO LEARN—NOW

Wait, that sounds an awful lot like paying your dues, doesn't it? To be sure, in some hard-charging jobs, being aggressive and getting your voice heard early and often (and even eschewing grunt work) might be a sign of a highflier. But those jobs are the exception, not the rule. Paying your dues these days isn't about getting coffee or kissing up to the boss. Instead, it's about understanding what you've been hired to do and getting it right day in and day out. It's about proving yourself in your primary role and learning to fit into the team and the broader corporate culture.

This doesn't mean selling out or being held back by old-school expectations from managers who have been working at the company before you were even born (although, these days, your manager is just as likely to be just a few years senior to you . . . more proof that getting the right things right can be rewarding). But it does mean understanding what exactly you were hired to do then figuring out how to be better at that job than anyone else.

The worst thing you could do at this early stage in your career is try to get by doing just the bare minimum in your real role while you bide your time to get to the good stuff, like actually writing and presenting the best-bet plan for the next big technology effort at your company. Expecting to make that leap before you've proven yourself in your current role because you believe you're infinitely more qualified than the guy doing the job now, or because you think your talents are being wasted behind the scenes, well . . . that's just unrealistic. Worse, it's likely to leave the impression that you want the glory but don't want to do what's necessary to earn it.

Take heart, the speed of business these days means that your prove-it period will be far shorter than it was for new hires from even a decade ago, and certainly far shorter than it was when your parents entered the workforce. That means once you've mastered the core of your job, you can—and should—ask to take on more responsibility. More on how to do that later, but first, you'll need to focus on making that critical first impression.

MAKING A GOOD FIRST IMPRESSION

The early days of a new job are critical for many reasons— they provide a strong footing for what's to come, for starters. But probably most important is the first impressions you make on a boss and your coworkers. It's human nature to size each other up quickly, be it pinpointing a professor as a tough assigner based on the first action-packed lecture or deciding a sports teammate is self-absorbed after a few ball-hogging incidents and little praise offered for teammates.

Notice these impressions have little to do with performance. That professor could be one of the best at the university, teaching you more than any other in your four years at the school. And the self-important teammate could be the

QUINTESSENTIAL FIRST IMPRESSION TIPS (ADAPTED FROM QUINTESSENTIAL CAREERS)[23]

Have a positive attitude. Nothing works better than having a positive attitude. Let your enthusiasm for being part of the team and the organization show. Leave nonwork problems at home.

Dress professionally/blend in with coworkers. Dress professionally—the way you want to be perceived. Being well groomed and well dressed signals efficiency and reliability to those around you and can lead to better assignments.

Learn coworkers' names quickly. Know the names of every member of your team. If you forget a person's name, simply apologize and ask the person's name again.

Ask questions/ask for help. No one expects you to solve all the organization's problems or to know everything on your first days on the job. Ask questions or ask for help when you need it.

Be a self-starter; take initiative. In most situations, in your first days on the job, you will be given small doses of work. As you finish assignments and are ready to handle a bigger workload, take the initiative and ask for more.

Work full days. There's nothing that can affect your reputation faster than routinely coming into work late or leaving early. Early on, get to work early and leave no earlier than when the majority of your coworkers leave.

Listen more than talk. You don't want to get the reputation as the office know-it-all or someone who always has to have the limelight. If you have a legitimate contribution, make it, but if not, do more listening and absorbing.

reason your team is in the semifinals this year instead of sitting at home after another near-miss for the playoffs. These impressions have to do with *personality*, and sometimes, performance-related traits actually matter *less* than the personality traits conveyed. The same is absolutely true for you and your new job. You could be technically superior to your fellow newbies—and maybe even some of your more experienced colleagues—but if you are a braggart or presumptive about your importance, that could outweigh everything else in the perception category.

Here's the good news: you aren't going to be expected to wow your bosses with your work those first few days or weeks (although doing so humbly is a big plus) so you can—and should—focus a lion's share of your attention on making a good personal impression and figuring out what's expected of you early on.

WHAT'S EXPECTED AND WHAT TO EXPECT

Figuring out what's expected of you all starts with strong communication. In some cases, what's expected of you in your new role will seem fairly clear. For example, if your boss tells you that you will be responsible for assisting a specific lead engineer and his team with modeling and testing for a new yearlong initiative around building a stronger widget in a certain category, that sounds pretty straightforward, right? Well, sort of. You know three things: for now you're beholden to a particular person (the lead engineer); you'll likely handle a good bit of modeling and testing; the goal for your team is a stronger widget.

There's a lot you still don't know, including how the team works; who does what in the group; what stage the project is in; what you'll be doing if, say, the testing phase has yet to begin; and how your performance will be judged. Even in companies that have set "plans" for employees for the first two years—such as investment banks like Goldman Sachs or

J.P. Morgan, where new analysts spend most of the first two years supporting higher-level bankers with spreadsheets, or consultancies like Booz Allen Hamilton or McKinsey, where junior consultants spend a year or so analyzing sales data and profit drivers for clients—the details of that work will vary by the group you work with.

How do you find this out? Observe quietly and, more important, ask. Too many young and new employees figure their bosses or colleagues will simply let them know if they're not doing something quite right. That's not always true and, besides, it's far better to take the initiative to find out yourself. Ask your boss or—in the example above, the lead engineer— what he wants to see from you on a consistent basis. What outcomes and results are expected from your work? What sort of information should you be providing and how often? Are there smaller key milestones or work expectations that you need to be mindful of? Can he help you define your performance and project objectives for the next six months (this will be important later for assessing your progress personally and with the boss)?

And finally, ask this: Is there anything else I should keep in mind or that I might not realize I need to be aware of or handle? This is an old reporter trick. Most of the best journalists and writers end every interview with this sort of question, and often the answer leads to an entirely new direction for a story, offers an even deeper understanding of the topic, or provides a stronger framework for how to think about an issue. Essentially, you want to get a handle on anything else you need to know. The question will usually prompt the boss to pause for a moment and, click, on goes a lightbulb in his head. Listen for how the answer impacts your work or office culture expectations (sometimes the answer will be a tip for dealing with a particularly difficult coworker or a tidbit about the small, but really important, part of your work responsibilities).

Okay, now you have a sense of what's expected of you. So what, exactly, should *you* expect from your first few weeks or months on the job? For starters, expect to be given small tasks to start, with bigger responsibilities and more high-stakes assignments coming your way as the weeks go on and your supervisors and colleagues develop trust in your work.

Just as you are learning your way around the office, tech systems, and flow of work, your bosses and colleagues are learning how you work and engaging in the delicate dance of figuring out how to fit your talents and quirks into the group. So, it might take a few weeks before the boss realizes he needn't check in with you several times a day to make sure you're on track—you can speed that up by keeping the boss informed about what you're doing, easing his mind that you are on track and signaling that you don't need as-frequent check-ins.

COPING WITH COMMON NEWBIE FRUSTRATIONS

You've been at the top of your class, the top of your fraternity or sorority, the top of, well, just about everything. You are used to being trusted, praised for your ideas, and handling your time and assignments without too much hand-holding or direction. That makes it doubly difficult for high-achieving young professionals to cope with some of the office norms and boss relations faced in a first professional job. But to build your career on a solid footing, it's important to deal with them—and get over it—quickly. Those who can't will surely find career progress to be slower in the first few years.

Here are several common frustrations you might feel—and ideas about how to turn the tables on them in a way that will help advance your career.

SHADOW BOSSES

In those early days on the job, a boss or higher-level colleague might double-check your work a bit too regularly, stand over your shoulder a bit too often, or ask to review one too many memos you send to a client or another department. Needless to say, this can feel pretty rotten—after all, weren't you hired because you were smart and capable of handling these assignments without being constantly watched? Most people would bristle at this sort of shadowing, but there are ways to not only end the close watch fairly quickly but also to use the behavior to your advantage.

For starters, try to think about this over-the-shoulder monitoring not as a lack of faith or trust in your abilities but rather as a way for a new boss or senior staffer to build the confidence in you that will result in your being given bigger, better work assignments to handle independently. One way to do that is to take control over check-ins by keeping your superiors informed—*before* they come to you. If you know the boss checks in twice a day, almost like clockwork, anticipate what he'll ask and send a quick note ahead of time letting him know where your work stands.

When you know your work is going to be double-checked, give a brief synopsis of how you conducted the assignment and ask—ahead of time—for feedback about anything that isn't spot-on or could be done in a different or better way. Approaching these situations with an attitude that shows you're both willing to learn and also trustworthy will not only help you lose your unwanted shadows quicker, but help you get more challenging work faster.

FEELING UNDERUTILIZED

For today's generation of do-more young adults, "faster, smarter, and with more creativity" is nearly a mantra. In the world of work—in many cases, anyway—you're likely to feel underutilized in the first few months. You might think you're capable of so much more than even the more-challenging work you've received after a month or two on the job. And you might be right. But figuring out when to broach the sub-

WHAT IF I HATE MY JOB?

What if, a few months into your first job, you've got a sinking feeling, per-haps even a tinge of depression. You hate the job but you're not sure why. It's a more common feeling than you might think. The key is to figure out what's bothering you. It could be that the job really is a bad fit. But in many cases, the first few months of any transition are simply hard to push through.

The Wall Street Journal offered this advice to new grads:

"Examine the duties of more-senior colleagues. Are their jobs appeal-ing? If so, stick out the entry-level drudgery in hopes of attaining more re-warding roles. But if the senior jobs also seem awful, that's a sign you're in the wrong career, company or job.

"Another strategy is to find a slightly older mentor at the company, coaches say. Ask that person: Did you go through this? Is this normal? When does it change, if at all?

"You should be prepared to accept some normal, and difficult, aspects of working life, coaches advise. For the first three to six months, expect to feel overwhelmed: Many tasks will be brand new, and you won't always un-derstand how your efforts fit into the bigger picture.

"Another thing recent grads struggle with is not having control over their schedules. Unless a first job is unbearably awful, coaches recommend grads persevere for six to 12 months."[24]

ject of underutilization and how to get more work without appearing—as many Gen Y-ers do—to feel as if you deserve to do more because you're simply better and smarter than what is required by the work on your plate now, is critical.

Expect to feel that your full capabilities aren't being tapped for the first month or two; toward the end of that time period, try approaching colleagues and the boss with an offer to volunteer to assist on other assignments or projects. In some cases, that will do the trick and make it apparent that you can handle more—and different—work. If you feel the same way beyond that timeframe, have a chat with your supervisor. Quickly review what you've accomplished and ask if you've missed the mark in any way. If the answer is no, simply tell the boss you're ready to do more and pinpoint exactly what skills you'd like to put to good use—and offer ideas on where. Doing so demonstrates knowledge of what's important to the team and your commitment to the work—both strong building blocks for your career and the networking and references you will need in the future.

Too-Helpful Colleagues

It's easy to get suspicious when your more experienced co-workers constantly offer their help or force it on you with their advice and personal work tips. Try to ride this out with a smile. It's almost always a product of good—not evil. That co-worker might have never received the help he needed when he was a newbie or might think the company is particularly hard for young employees to navigate and sees himself doing his part to make your life easier. Your best bet is to listen, absorb, and occasionally take the advice, but keep thinking for yourself. Remember that your helpful colleague might have been a newbie in totally different conditions.

You should take any tips to heart, whether on how to judge the boss's mood; the best way to talk to a client; preferred formats for memos, spreadsheets and the like; or on great local lunch spots or where to get the good pens or corporate discount cards. Rejecting the person outright could be seen as being a know-it-all. So try if someone is trying to help you, let him or her help with things you really need to know, such as the location of the conference room for that meeting you've got to be at in five minutes or how to pronounce the managing director's complicated last name. If a too helpful colleague gets to be too much to handle, after a few weeks, you can politely shoo him away with your work

PHONE SKILLS MATTER

Cubicles are a very public place to learn your job. Chances are the people around you can hear everything. That means when you make a rookie mistake on the phone with a client or someone else, it's likely someone else will hear it, which makes matters that much worse. Common flubs: misstating industry lingo, leaving rambling messages, or sounding inarticulate. Trouble is, you're actually more likely to make a mistake if you are nervous because you feel your coworkers might be listening. Eventually, you'll feel more self-confident. Meanwhile, here are some tips for coping:

Come in early or stay late. You can make calls without many of your colleagues around and ratchet down your nerves. Even if you don't reach the person, you've made the initial contact and can leave messages without fear of being overheard—and inadvertently tripping up because of it. If your coworkers generally go to lunch at around the same time, make your calls then.

Use a headset. You can move your hands around freely, just as you might if you were in a face-to-face conversation with someone. This can make you feel more at ease.

Find privacy. For the most anxiety-inducing calls, you should look for a private office or other location to make your calls, at least until you feel more sure of yourself.

Start small. If you have to make a series of similar calls to multiple people, start with the least important person. If you fumble a bit, it's less likely to be noticed and you'll be practiced enough that the call to a more important person should go smoothly.[25]

commitments: "Joe, you give me great tips, but I've got to get this to the boss in an hour and my next deadline is at the end of the day and if I don't focus, I'll never finish." Then look back down at your work and get to it.

BUILDING A RELATIONSHIP WITH THE BOSS

In most jobs—and especially in your first post-college job—your relationship with your boss is the most important one you will build. This is the relationship that can either put you on the fast track for future success . . . or set you back in your professional career. Ask any successful professional whose shoes you aspire to be in someday, and it's almost certain she'll tell you about a boss who helped pave the way to career success—and most likely is still a mentor or friend who continues to give advice and make connections, even decades later.

What's more, there's today to think about. Your boss is the person you probably interact with most on the day to day: the person who reviews your work, recommends you for assignments and promotions, and can be either an asset, mentor, and champion or the roadblock that keeps you from enjoying your work and getting to the next level. Very early on, your boss will size you up and decide if you're top-tier, middle-of-the-pack, or just okay. Part of that assessment will be squarely about your actual work. But the rest—as numerous psychology texts and studies have discovered—is largely a matter of how you get along and the personal connection the boss feels toward you.

You've done your homework, so you should already know a little bit about what the boss is like and what he or she expects of you in the job. Now it's time to build more than just an acceptable working relationship, one in which your boss will actually *want* to champion you and your work—the sort of long-lasting genuine relationship that will propel your career. To be sure, it helps to have a boss who takes an interest in your success from the start. But even if he doesn't do that right away, a lukewarm boss can quickly become an asset if you work at building the relationship. Here's how:

Be the Right Kind of Asset

Let's face it, if you do your job well, it makes your boss's job easier. So first things first: excel at the work on your plate, deliver results and materials on time and correctly, perform to the best of your ability, and work to solve problems and get questions answered without the need for constant handholding (question asking is fine, but remember, first try your coworkers or senior staffers). Knowing she doesn't have to keep an eagle eye on your work or progress is a silent sigh of relief for a boss and immediately makes you an asset, mostly because you make her life easier.

Now, for step two. Watch the boss for cues of what she needs done that either isn't getting done right or quickly enough by other people. If you're qualified and able, offer to help (as long as you won't be seen as trying to upstage a colleague or step on someone's toes). Or offer to take on other work that might be lower priority but still needs to be done, so she can focus on the more critical tasks at hand. Relieving your boss of the small stuff might not always be exciting, but it builds incredible goodwill and trust. It also sets you apart from colleagues who might just want to work on the glory projects and assignments—and makes it more likely you'll get those.

Master the Boss's Work Style

Does your boss spend the first hour of the day responding to e-mails or prepping for a daily meeting? Does he seem stressed or particularly busy between the hours of 10 a.m. and noon but more relaxed after lunch? Does he regularly communicate via e-mail or is he the type that likes to speak face-to-face, except for the simplest of communications? Is he a stickler for procedure or a try-it-and-see-what-sticks type?

These are important things to observe, understand, and adapt to. You will not ingratiate yourself to the boss if you pepper him with questions or office pop-ins during the time of day he likes to be left alone to handle e-mails. You will not only annoy him but have less success than if you approach your boss during the times he's least busy or, at least, the most open to consultation—so it pays to figure out when that is. Finally, if your boss is an e-mailer and you're a talker, try to conform. If he's a face-to-face communicator and you get nervous in such situations, practice it in less nerve-racking conditions, perhaps by walking up to a peer or slightly more senior coworker to chat about a task at hand, instead of e-mailing.

Follow Through, Without Fail

There are two sides to the coin. On one side, there's the work that has a hard deadline and clear deliverables. Get those things done on time, every time. That's just common sense, right? If you don't do this basic of the job, your boss not only won't be your ally but he probably won't see much of a reason to keep you in the job. And then there are the things you don't need to inform your boss that you've completed (unless he asks you to). For example, if you're responsible for writing the agenda for the Monday-afternoon meeting, you don't need to e-mail your boss Monday morning to tell him the agenda will be ready. He should be able to assume it will be ready, and he should be right every time.

Now, for the less obvious side of the coin. There will be plenty of things mentioned in passing that you agree to do . . . you know, the last words of a meeting, "Yes, we should look into that. When you have time, could you look up what it would take to do X and send me a note?" You nod your head yes and go back to work. These quasi-assignments are the things you do want to inform your boss that you've completed. Put the tasks on your work calendar and complete them quickly. Send a note to the boss the next day reminding him that you're looking into it and that you expect to have some information for him within a specific number of days. Why not just tell the boss you'll do it right then and there, before you walk back to your desk? You've heard the advice to underpromise and overdeliver, right? But it's a hard concept to internalize, especially for driven young go-getters.

You might think this in-passing assignment will take a certain amount of time, perhaps a few hours. Then once you start digging in, you realize you're going to need more time. Better to take a few minutes to size up the work—to give yourself a cushion—before making a commitment you can't follow through with. And always, always follow through on in-passing requests.

TAKE A PERSONAL INTEREST

Your boss is human, too. Surprised? But seriously, try to remember your boss is a person (one hopes), with a family, outside interests, as well as the weaknesses and frustrations that we all have. If you figure out the human side and attempt to relate to the boss as a *person* and not just a superior, you'll find the work side of things will often be significantly smoother. Take note of family photos and references to outside interests in your conversations (or chats the boss has with others). If, for example, you hear that your boss's son is playing in a soccer tournament over the weekend, on Monday ask him how the team did. Just don't overdo it, or you might come off as too nosy or invasive. You should also be willing to share (edited) tidbits about your own life, particularly where you and the boss share common interests or backgrounds. And don't forget to show your human side, too (including that winning sense of humor).

Little things like this build rapport and will also help you humanize the boss so that when, say, he's being a jerk because he's having a bad day, you'll be sympathetic rather than resentful. This will also pay off down the road when *you* need some slack or miss a deadline for personal reasons (as long as you let the boss know ahead of time, apologize, and quickly make up for the delays). What's more, if a slice of the relationship is personal, you're likely to score the golden reference booster of "She's a great person to work with" when you go for your next gig.

COMMUNICATE CLEARLY

It's very easy to get so wrapped up in your work that you forget to communicate with the boss often enough. Setting up reminder notes on your work calendar can help you stay organized. But it will take a bit more work to make sure you communicate clearly. A miscommunication once or twice is generally not going to be a problem, but failure to communicate clearly—or to make sure you understand the boss's comments clearly—on a regular basis is likely to irritate a boss and make her wonder why you don't get it.

When you get an assignment that's not completely clear, or if you're working on a complex or confusing project, repeat back the work you're being asked to do. Simply say, "Okay, I'm working on X. Just to be clear, I need to do Y, using W method and consulting with Z work we've done in the past." A response of yes lets you know you're on the right track. On the flip side, when you check in with the boss, be clear about what you've done or what you're working on. You don't need to go on at length in detail, but rather be concise. Vague language can lead to the sorts of miscommunications you don't want. Clarity signals reliability and comprehension.

OWN UP TO MISTAKES

There's not much explanation needed here. But all too often, young professionals are embarrassed or worried about the consequences if they admit a mistake or problem. And trust

WHEN THE BOSS IS IMPOSSIBLE

There are some bosses who, for a variety of reasons, are just bad to work for and difficult to build a relationship with. Some managers simply lack people skills. They may have been promoted for their technical prowess or their own successes as an employee, but never mastered the people part of the management equation. Other bosses rule with an iron fist or are quick to accuse or pass the buck to junior employees who've yet to build clout and reputation in the company. Still others stifle creativity by insisting even the simplest things be done their way—even if there's a faster, better, or more accurate way to handle whatever the task might be. Equally frustrating are those good bosses who are hard to reach, those senior people who are under tremendous stress and have little time to develop the kind of relationship you want—and need—to propel your career.

Don't worry, your career isn't dead in the water if you can't form a strong relationship with your boss. Instead, look to more senior colleagues or a department head whom you have experience with and work to develop ties with these more-willing professionals. They'll be able to serve as a reference when you look for your next job and—if they're respected within the company more broadly—even help pave the way for you to move up in the firm or get your boss to recognize your future value, too. A well-timed note from a respected colleague or another senior manager to your boss about a recent assignment you hit out of the park can only help.

me, you will make a mistake or two in your first year on the job (and probably in the future as you take on new challenges). But hiding or minimizing any error is the worst thing you can do, and the consequences of doing so will almost always be far greater than owning up right away.

Instead, quickly go to your boss—in person—explain the mistake, and tell him what you're doing to remedy the error. The boss might still be livid if the mistake has a ripple effect, but not as mad as he would be if you said nothing or minimized the issue—or worse, tried to blame someone else. Act fast and have a solution or fix you can implement just as quickly. Everyone makes mistakes, but you never want the boss to hear about yours from someone else. That will only serve to cause the boss to call into question the rest of your work and dismantle the trust you've worked so hard to build.

Take Feedback Seriously

When you get feedback from your boss about your work, whether it's a formal review or a casual comment in passing, it can be tempting to just listen for the positive and make mental excuses for any negatives (you know what I'm talking about: the little voice that says, "That's only a problem because my project coworkers slacked off," or "Oh, that's such a small thing, it's no big deal"). Don't succumb to this. Instead, listen for areas of where you can improve and then vow to develop a personal strategy for getting better in areas of weakness or simply ratcheting up your work a notch.

You never want to receive the same less-than-positive feedback twice. If the boss says your grammar in the memos that accompany your excellent spreadsheet analyses needs some work, he shouldn't have to say it again in two weeks. The first time you get a critique, ask for details or specifics about what you are doing wrong, and ask if you can be pointed to a colleague whose memos are up to snuff then ask that person for examples. You could also look outside the company for resources to help you improve a certain skill; in this case, for example, you could buy a book on grammar or take a course in business writing. Developing a new skill doesn't happen overnight, so in the meantime you may, for example, want to have a colleague whose command of grammar is better than yours review your next note before you hit the Send button.

GETTING AND USING FEEDBACK TO YOUR ADVANTAGE

What sets apart many successful young professionals—and puts them on the fast track—is an ability to get meaningful feedback, understand it, and use it to improve their work. After all, the way we progress in our careers in some part depends on what others (especially bosses) think about our work and our professional demeanor.

But it can be hard to get honest feedback—or at least the kind that is useful, actionable, and career-building. Research repeatedly shows that most supervisors play down negative feedback (although there are plenty of anecdotes about bosses who do just the opposite) or fail to pinpoint how subordinates could improve, even if they are clear about areas for improvement. That makes getting good feedback something you have to work at, rather than expect to come at regular intervals.

Speaking of regular intervals, all too often feedback comes at scheduled reviews six months into a job and again at the one-year mark. In some companies, there's more "official" feedback and at others, that once-a-year meeting is the only formalized review you'll get. That is, unless you ask for more and deploy a strategy for picking up on informal feedback from the superiors and senior staffers you regularly work with. In fact, the most useful feedback you get will likely be from informal information you get by, well, asking and listening. As important, recognize that the most useful feedback you get might not be from your boss, but from a close colleague or senior staffer.

The hardest part of feedback is often accepting it. Many people are really looking for approval when they ask for feedback. But what they need is real constructive criticism and information. Many young professionals learn the hard way that the way people perceive their work and their personality is far different from what they believe about themselves. You might think you're an aggressive person who gets things done; your coworkers might see you as a bully who doesn't listen to smaller voices. You might think you're doing a great job of servicing a client because you answer e-mails promptly and deliver projects on time. That client might see your quickness as not taking the time to think about the needs behind the words of an e-mail or proposal. You might see yourself as willing to go to whatever lengths needed to see a project through. Others might say you are someone who overdoes everything he touches.

This is why it's critical to be open to the idea that what you hear when you ask for feedback might be at odds with what you believe about yourself. It's all about adjusting your perception. Often, a few small tweaks to your behavior and work will push the needle of perception toward the way you see yourself.

Here's how to get the kind of feedback that will benefit your career:

WHOM TO ASK FOR FEEDBACK

Seems like a dumb question, right? You want feedback from the boss. After all, he's the one who approves the raises and submits those formal reviews. It's true that you want the boss's input. But sometimes you can get equally valuable—and more immediately usable—feedback from a coworker or someone you work with tangentially.

Identify several coworkers whose work you admire and who have a reputation of impressing the higher-ups with their work. This could be a peer a few years your senior whom you are regularly teamed with or a junior manager who receives out-loud praise for his skills. The people you want feedback from should be colleagues or superiors you'd like to emulate and whose work is close enough to what you do—or want to do—that what you learn from them will be useful.

How to Ask for Feedback

First, you need to make sure you've done enough actual work to ask for input about it. You can ask for feedback before you have finished a project, particularly if it is important or the first time you've been through the particular exercise. Just make sure you're far enough along and have double-checked your work first. In this case, you can ask your trusted colleague or a senior staffer if he has a moment to look at what you've done and offer any suggestions.

Be specific about what you want to know. Don't just ask the person to tell you what they think about your work. Instead, you might ask if anything seems to be missing or if he can offer some insight on a specific piece of the project he might be knowledgeable about. Start with something like this: "Joe, your projects are always spot-on and this is my first one of this kind. I feel like part three might be a little off target. Would you mind taking a look at this and letting me know what I could do to sharpen my analysis?"

If a project or assignment has just wrapped up, asking for feedback is more nuanced. You want to get something useful. To do that, try beginning with a small criticism of yourself. You might say, "I think I could have done a better job building the analysis on part three. Your analysis is always spot-on. What's your secret? What might I be missing or doing wrong?" This will make the person you ask feel both a little flattered and more comfortable being honest. Plus, it identifies a specific area of feedback need.

So how formal do you want your request to be? It depends. Casual requests can sometimes garner the quickest immediate (and honest) feedback. But if you want to have a chance to really sit down with a person and delve into the specifics, you need to ask for a more formal meeting. If this is the case, make sure to be direct and specific in your reasons for asking. "I'd like to do a postmortem on the project, if you have fifteen minutes sometime in the next few days. Since I'm still new at this, I'd like to hear your thoughts about areas where I could improve, like in part three where the analysis I was doing is new territory for me."

LISTENING FOR HIDDEN PERFORMANCE CLUES

Some of the useful feedback you'll get in your career will come to you quite indirectly, often when you least expect it, which means you'll need to develop an ear for hearing what will most likely be disguised in regular conversation or passing comment. That makes it important to know what to listen—and watch—for.

First, learn to read the body language of your boss and senior colleagues. You'll quickly be able to recognize when he's stressed out, in a bad mood, or particularly pleased with something.

Those extreme moods are easier to spot, though, than the more subtle hints about the small stuff. When your supervisor is in one of those easily noticed moods, look at his facial expressions (is he looking away, is his temple pulsing, does he have big smile, is he skeptical with an upturned eyebrow?) and the way he holds himself (is he slumped or standing straight up, flailing his hands as he speaks or calm and relaxed behind the desk). Remember those cues. Later, when the boss is talking about your latest proposal or analysis, take note of the body language you see and mentally compare it to those obvious moods.

If you catch one of these nonverbal cues, say a raised eyebrow or a pulsing temple, albeit less noticeably, take a second to think about why your boss is reacting this way. What about the work you're discussing could be frustrating him or making him skeptical? If you're not sure, stop and ask. If you're discussing your analysis of the marketing plan for a new product and you get the raised eyebrow, you might say, "I sense some skepticism; is there something I might have missed?"

Off-the-cuff feedback can be just as hard to tune your ear to as body language can sometimes be, but knowing when you're hearing an important message isn't just valuable in your relationship with the boss or your peers. It's also a skill that will serve you well throughout your career—from listening to junior staffers who might not always come out and say what they mean but have something important to say, to people you interview with for your next job whose word choices could point you to a better answer.

Listen for toss-out comments at the end of a conversation or meeting that clue you in. Did your coworker who said your work looks good follow that by saying you could also have used another formula to do your analysis that the higher-ups like? That doesn't necessarily mean you should jump to do the analysis with the other formula. But it is worth a quick note or chat with the boss about his preference (so you don't get that raised eyebrow later). Most indirect feedback will come as asides at the end of conversations or as the "but" in an otherwise positive exchange. Knowing your workplace culture—and the expectations and sticking points of your boss and colleagues—will clue you in to whether any tidbit or "but" requires a real change, an inquiry, or nothing at all.

USING CRITICISM AND FEEDBACK TO IMPROVE YOUR WORK

Remember, above all, feedback is not usually personal. Rather, it's a tool to assess and improve your work and, ultimately, your performance and your career. Once you internalize that fact, you can put the feedback you get to good use to improve your work. That doesn't mean every bit of feedback needs to be taken to heart and acted upon immediately, although direct criticism from the boss or a supervisor on a project should be. When evaluating feedback from peers, it's wise to consider any built-in bias in a peer's perspective and/ or his knowledge of the area before adopting any change.

HOW TO RECOVER
FROM A BAD FORMAL REVIEW

Nobody wants to hear that they aren't doing something well—or as well as they thought. That's particularly true during the formal review process. The issue is more likely to be in writing and require quicker, specific action to improve. It's very easy to get defensive and ultimately miss out on an opportunity to quickly address the issue and impress the bosses well before your next formal review. Remember, in most cases, a "bad" review won't be *all* bad. Look at it as a chance to turn things around. Follow these steps to take what you need from what you're hearing—and quickly recover:

- Be open-minded and willing to self-assess. What you are hearing is usually meant to help you do your job better, not to trash your work. Don't debate the validity of what you're told; instead, listen and ask for clarification and specifics about areas of improvement. Acknowledge that you understand what you've just heard and—hard as it might be—thank your boss for the feedback.[26]

- With clarity about what needs improvement, develop a plan to address the corresponding areas of your work. It might help to discuss what you've heard and your ideas for improving with a mentor or a close colleague or friend. If it's a specific technical skill that needs work, look for a class or an internal expert you can turn to.

- Meet with the boss within a few days to go over how you plan to improve and ask if he has suggestions to alter your plan or if there's a particular colleague who is very good in the area you are working on. If you've identified a course you think would help, ask if you can attend.

- As you have evidence of your progress, check in with the boss. If, for example, the negative feedback was about your less-than-professional-sounding memos and e-mails to people in other parts of the company, forward your improved communications and ask the boss if you're on the right track.

- If you receive praise or positive feedback from someone else in the area your boss cited for improvement, relay that to the boss with a repeated thanks for pointing out this trouble spot and a tip to the idea that you hope this positive feedback is a strong sign that you took the problem seriously and have worked to improve.

If you need to, ask for clarification about the insights you've been given. If a colleague says you could sharpen your presentation, ask how or what you could do better. Don't be defensive; you're not asking for your colleague to defend his thoughts, but, rather, to give you an example that you can take back and actually work on. Do you need to improve your technical skills in something specific? Look for a class through HR or find an online instructional program—and then take it to heart and practice. Are your presentation skills not up to snuff because you're not direct with the audience? Ask a coworker (or a friend) to help you practice in advance next time.

In some cases, you'll receive feedback that's more difficult to integrate into your everyday work. If the boss says you need to do a better job connecting the dots and synthesizing information—essentially, stronger critical thinking—your best bet is to regularly step back from a particular project or assignment and try to look at the bigger picture. In these more abstract improvement areas, ask the boss or a trusted colleague for a regular (temporary) check-in to see how you're doing and get specifics to keep improving. Sometimes, the less-tangible comes only with time and experience. Most supervisors know and understand that.

And don't ignore positive feedback. After all, you were hired because you were among the best and brightest and have a lot to offer the company. Listen to the good stuff and figure out how you can do more of it, either in the same way or applied to different tasks and assignments you handle. If you've been told your memos are always articulate and on target, think of ways you can use those qualities in other parts of your work—perhaps as the backbone of how you put together your first client presentation.

A WORD ABOUT MENTORS

Actually, make that four critical words: you need a mentor. Why? Mentors have experience and knowledge that you need. They've been there, done that. They've made the mistakes you might be about to make, they've navigated the career ladder and made it up to rungs you hope to reach. They've also done the kind of work and made the kind of career moves you're making now, which puts them in just the right place to ask you whether you've tried a different technique that has worked for them or whether you've looked into certain training or departments you might not have considered. They can also start a lot of sentences with "When I was in a similar situation, this is what I did/tried/realized. . . ."

Not convinced? Career coaches and experts say young professionals with good mentor relationships are often able to navigate their early careers more successfully than their counterparts without mentors and have access to career opportunities more frquently (and often earlier than peers with weak or no mentor relationships). Mentors are established professionals who've successfully built their careers, are not your boss, and who are available to you for building a level of trust and openness that you need in order to wade through the early years (and really, most of the years) of your career. What's more, you need to be connected to people like that not just for the guidance and insights you can gain from them but also because in a successful mentor relationship, you will eventually be able to tap into your sage's professional network.

WHAT IF I DON'T LIKE MY ASSIGNED MENTOR?

This was a question posed to the *Wall Street Journal*'s "Career Q&A" column more than once. A bad mentor-mentee match can present a number of issues, not the least of which is an unproductive relationship. For young professionals, asking for a different mentor can seem daunting; after all, you don't want to offend anyone or seem overly picky. Plus, you're new at the mentor thing and might think you just need to give it time. But if your mentor really isn't working out for whatever reason, trust your instincts and don't be afraid to speak up and look for guidance elsewhere. Here are some tips adapted from *The Wall Street Journal*'s "Career Q&A":

- Look outside official mentor channels for career guidance. Some of the most helpful mentors don't come from formal programs, but rather from people whom you seek out or befriend (or vice versa).

- Recognize that in-house mentoring programs have specific goals in mind, and they often don't mesh with what a mentee might hope to achieve. For the company, a formal program is often designed to nurture promising employees, while many young professionals want specific guidance and a relationship that can help fast-track their careers, says Sherri Thomas, president of Career Coaching 360.

- Look for ways to get something out of the formal mentor arrangement. Home in on areas of influence, skill set, or the key traits of your assigned mentor that can help you. This won't work in the case of a disinterested mentor, but for others, you can still get a few key tips or pointers.

- If formal mentoring is a big deal in your firm and you do not like your mentor, ask to be reassigned. Before you do, write up a short list of reasons—avoiding accusatory or blanket language—you'd like a new mentor and a clear list of what you'd like to get out of a mentor relationship. Offer suggestions about the type of person you want to be paired with (just realize not everyone gets a senior-level manager as their mentor; people a few rungs down the ladder can be more helpful and have more influence over senior managers).[27]

About 70 percent of Fortune 500 companies offer a formal or semiformal mentoring program of some kind. At International Business Machines Corp., for example, every employee is assigned a "connection coach" before his or her first day; after they join, workers are assigned a formal mentor.[28]

Mentoring programs have become a popular way for companies to help grow high-potential younger staffers and, at higher levels, groom their next generation of leaders. Typically, employees are paired with more senior employees at their company who have some commonality.[29]

Some programs offer clear guidance on how to develop the relationship and have executives monitor the mentoring success rate (or areas for improvement) diligently. In other cases, the company's role largely ends after making a match and some occasional check-ins. Without some clear guidelines, however, such arranged relationships are prone to fizzle out more quickly.

WHAT KIND OF MENTOR DO I NEED?

While formal mentor programs can vary in quality and helpfulness, it's useful to be involved simply for the exposure it offers to people outside your direct group. And, you can—and in many cases should—still find a separate mentor outside the program. These days, developing a relationship with a career sage takes more legwork than it has in the past. The economic downturn and slow recovery, coupled with a skepticism about the commitment of Millennials in the workplace, have made mentors a bit harder to find and grow. That just means you need to be more strategic about choosing a mentor and cultivating the relationship.

The first thing you need to do is determine your personal mentoring goals. What do you want to gain from a mentor? Do you want to learn more about project management? Are you interested in learning about the people side of the business? Do you want help navigating corporate politics? Make a list of those goals and stack them based on their priority level. If finding your way through the murky sea of office politics is key to succeeding at the firm—and you aren't good at it—that should be your No. 1 goal.

Note that you're not looking for a mentor to help you develop a specific technical skill set. Think of your mentor more like a career guide with less of the pressure and awkwardness that comes with getting such guidance from your direct supervisor. After all, you'll want insights on workplace issues and getting ahead, which could mean strategies for dealing with your boss.

You should also consider your personality and communication style. Are you introverted and wish you could be more outgoing? You'll want to add *outgoing* to a list of hoped-for qualities in a mentor. Or perhaps you're extroverted and quick to raise your hand to answer a question. Consider a mentor who is more measured and thoughtful (a quality that isn't necessarily at odds with quick to answer, but rather a trait that is often appreciated as you climb the corporate ladder). If you're someone who prefers face-to-face interaction, you'll want to avoid a mentor whose management communication style is known to be e-mail-only.

Once you have a good understanding of what you want in a mentor, look for a colleague who has had the experiences or the knowledge (or the career track) that align with what you'd like to acquire or learn. Remember that a good mentor doesn't need to be an executive or someone five levels above you. Sometimes the best guide will be one or two levels above you or someone at a similar level in another department. The higher up your hoped-for mentor, the less likely he'll have a lot of time to spend with you. That doesn't mean you should eliminate that executive you admire from your list, but be realistic and supplement with others who are likely to have more time for hands-on attention.

Before you approach the person, ask someone who knows her style about how the potential mentor might respond to your request and ask about her work style. Keep in mind you need at least one mentor who has the potential to guide you down the career path you'd like to follow—someone who has roughly followed the path you want to be on and who has been recognized for her work along the way. When you have more than one mentor—and as your career progresses, it's likely that you will—you should be very specific about what you hope to gain from each relationship; too much input from too many people on the same topics or situations can have a paralyzing effect and leave you confused about what to do.

THE BIG ASK: SECURING A MENTOR

Perhaps the thought of asking someone to mentor you feels a bit like asking your high school crush to go to the movies for the first time. Awkward, right? Maybe, but if you aren't part of a formal mentoring program at work—or if you are but still want some guidance from someone else, too—there's no way around it: you'll have to ask. Exactly how to do so depends on how well you know the person already, what you hope to gain, and how formal your company culture is.

The indirect direct approach. One technique: if you have worked with the person or already been in contact for other reasons, you could approach the person you'd like to learn from informally, but with a specific, single request in mind. You could, for example, tell a respected manager that you admire his work and ask him if he might have time over the next few months to coach you on something specific, like how to close on a big sale or how to engage colleagues on a project. By the time that project is over, you'll likely have forged a relationship that will naturally continue and grow.

If you're seeking mentorship from someone you know only tangentially or have admired from afar, take it a little slower. Being asked face-to-face for guidance by someone you've never met or heard of can be off-putting (imagine how you'd feel). Instead, send an e-mail explaining how you know of the person's work and why you admire it and requesting advice on a very specific issue (think something like "Because of your expertise in this area and your knowledge of how things operate here, I hope you don't mind me asking how you'd suggest handling X").

Then, gauge the person's response. Was it relatively quick and helpful? Did it seem to invite further conversation? If so, you can follow up with gratitude and an offer to buy the person lunch or coffee (at which point you can be more direct about asking if you can come back for guidance or insights again). Or, simply respond with a big thank-you and ask if it would be okay to contact him again for advice on such matters. After a couple of positive exchanges, ask directly if this person would consider mentoring you more formally. When you ask, be sure you know what you mean by "more formally" and quickly describe how you'd see the relationship working. For example, you might say something like "We could meet once or twice a month and work through some specific goals similar to the things you have already been helpful with. And maybe we could touch base in between if needed. I'll be respectful of your time; I know you're busy."

A more direct ask. If the person you want to mentor you is someone you've worked with or already received casual guidance from—someone who knows you a bit already—you might already consider him an informal mentor or go-to guide. Formalizing the relationship is still important. But you can be more direct than you can be with someone you barely know.

Tell your would-be sage that you admire his work and have grown to consider him a critical informal mentor. Then say something like "As a newbie in this company and on the career ladder, I've appreciated all I've learned from you so far and your career path is one I might like to emulate. Would you consider mentoring me more formally?" Again, quickly explain how you see the relationship working.

With either approach, it's best to have enough knowledge about the person, his work, and his management style (and if possible, a sense of how he is viewed as a mentor to others). This will make it easier on your nerves to ask for guidance and keep you from getting that puzzled, oh-boy-that-was-out-of-left-field, who-is-this-kid look.

KEYS TO SUCCESSFUL MENTOR-MENTEE RELATIONSHIPS

Success in your mentoring relationships depends in large part on laying groundwork for the relationship from the start. It might feel a bit too formal doing that at first, but setting the general rules will pave the way for a more fluid and easy relationship going forward. At the beginning of the relationship, mentoring partners should clearly discuss the logistics of how the relationship will work. Will you have a standing date to meet once or twice a month? Will you meet in the office or over lunch? Does your mentor want to get a sense of what you'll want to tackle before you meet? Will it be okay to check in between sessions if something comes up that your mentor could clearly offer guidance with? In most cases, it will also make sense to agree on a medium-term goal at the outset, say, learning a different side of the business or getting exposure to a different specialty. You can also develop short-term goals relevant to your job, group, or soft-skills development.

INFORMAL AND FORMAL MENTOR RELATIONSHIPS

Early in your career, it will be important to have some level of formal mentoring. But informal mentoring will often become something you rely on more as you progress in your career. For many people, some of their best informal mentorships are formed early on—perhaps even during an internship. Most informal mentoring relationships are born out of a good work relationship with a former supervisor or senior colleague or with someone with whom you share a common outside interest (say, surfing or marathon running, or a certain volunteer organization). An informal mentor could be a peer whose work you admire or who seems to have some personal and work style traits you'd like to adopt.

These relationships—really quasi-friendships—lend themselves to a level of immediate, implicit trust that formal mentoring only develops over time. An informal mentor is someone you can go to with the same sorts of issues you would a formal mentor, but also with stickier issues, including burgeoning concerns about fit, mushier work-life goals, and specific personality issues you're working through with your peers or bosses.

What's more, while formal mentoring often starts with a designated time frame for working together or on a specific issue and a more regimented schedule, informal mentors often offer more off-the-cuff advice seeking and more personal interjections (and since you have a more personal relationship to start, you're more likely to accept unsolicited constructive criticism).

Two other key differences: informal mentoring relies on a sort of chemistry between you and your mentor. You just click. You feel a personal bond and trust is developed immediately and is often implicit. Formal mentoring relies more on a sense of compatibility, in other words, pairing of two people whose personal and work styles are well matched (even if they aren't similar) to the point that they can work together to reach a common goal or set of goals and build a sense of trust along the way. Informal mentor relationships can exist between people of the same or different professional levels and at times, mentee becomes mentor. Formal mentor programs pair a more-seasoned manager or professional with a junior staffer in a much more structured way, similar to a teacher-student relationship.

In most cases, even a mentoring relationship that starts formally will develop over time to a point where there'll be less need for as formalized an approach. Chatting will come more easily and you'll gradually be comfortable contacting your mentor on an as-needed basis. Even so, keep that monthly check-in on the calendar to avoid drifting out of the relationship. Here are several other things to keep in mind to get the most out of mentoring:

Be personable. You should also take some time to get to know each other personally and professionally before tackling specific issues. Spending time discussing work styles, personalities, and personal backgrounds builds trust that will pay off later. And be yourself, not just a ladder-climbing young professional with only the next promotion on her mind. Remember that having access to a mentor is just the start. You want your mentors to feel invested in your success and career development. That means the person on the other side of the table needs to grow to like you, which doesn't happen in one or two meetings.

Give back. What's more, in most cases, that invested feeling won't happen if you're just in it for yourself. You might think you don't have very much to offer, but mentoring is a two-way street. Perhaps your mentor wants to learn something you know more about than he does, like how to use Twitter or set up a Facebook page or LinkedIn group. The best way to find out: ask. In those early meetings as you go over your goals, ask your mentor if there's anything he'd like to get from the relationship and offer up a few ideas.

You're also much more likely to work well with someone if "you're seen as someone who understands the pressures [a manager is] experiencing," says Thomas J. DeLong, an organizational behavior professor at Harvard Business School. Take stock of skills you have that match your mentor's workload and occasionally offer to pitch in on the side.

Think—and ask—smart. When it comes to scheduled meetings with your mentor, always show up prepared. Mentors—particularly in more formal mentoring relationships—are typically better at giving specific feedback or advice than they would be at, say, helping you brainstorm ideas or answer open-ended questions (think, "I've been thinking about asking to work with group X to get some exposure to Y. Do you think that's a good idea? How would you recommend asking my boss without upsetting protocol?" versus the less-succinct "I want to get exposure to more areas of the company. What do you think?").

Your specific questions are very likely to lead to broader discussions about the topic or even serve as a departure point for other issues. But to get the most out of a mentor relationship, you need to take responsibility for asking smart questions, particularly in the beginning, before the relationship takes on a more natural flow. This is all part of the small stuff involved in getting a mentor invested in your success!

Make sure you use your time wisely. Don't ask questions you could easily answer on your own or seek guidance on topics your mentor is unlikely to be able to offer insight about. If you've got a set agenda or even a loose commitment to talk about, say, managing a tricky interdepartmental project, it's probably best to avoid detailed questions about the project itself (unless your mentor is known to be a go-to resource for this sort of work). Instead, ask how she handled the politics or competing demands of interdepartmental work in the past.

Don't forget the tricky stuff. One topic that's often a good one to work through with a mentor: speaking up in awkward situations. For example, when you're early in a career or a job, it's easy to feel like you don't have room to speak up about conflicting directions or departmental silos that impact the results of a project. Guidance from a mentor who has been-there, done-that on the right way to interject or deflect can work wonders. But before you follow the advice to the

HOW DO I KNOW IF IT'S WORKING?

QuintCareers.com has summed it up nicely:

You'll know if the mentoring relationship is working if your mentor encourages your goals, provides honest and constructive feedback, helps you develop self-awareness, challenges you to grow beyond your perceived limitations, introduces you to movers and shakers, motivates you to join professional organizations that can help you advance, and above all, listens to you and is easy to communicate with.

Your mentor can help you assess your strengths and weaknesses, as well as help you develop skills for success and a long-range career plan. If you and your mentor share the same employer, your mentor can foster your sense of belonging within the organization, help you navigate the company culture and politics, as well as let you know who the organization's key players are. You can also work through career and workplace problems with your mentor's assistance.

A mentor can provide a fresh perspective—a new way of looking at a problem or issue. You can bounce ideas off your mentor. Look for a relationship in which the mentor is more coach than advisor—one in which the mentor facilitates your decision-making process by suggesting alternatives rather than telling you what to do. Ideally, your mentor will motivate you to do your best work.[30]

letter, consider the individual personalities involved and tailor how you implement the tips.

Express appreciation. Your mentor is likely to contribute more to the relationship than you will, particularly at first. Down the road, you might be giving back just as much by, say, offering up a contact of your own, lending a hand on a big project, or giving the perspective of a Millennial for a presentation your mentor is giving to the CEO. But for the time being, it's important to express gratitude to your mentor and make sure she knows you value her insights and guidance. A simple note of thanks with a few details about how you implemented her advice successfully is a good start. If your mentor has gone out of her way and the relationship is part of a formal company mentorship program, consider sending a note to the program coordinator. It's also okay to, say, bake cookies or bring a treat from time to time or offer to pick up the tab for coffee or lunch.

What you get from a mentor—now and later. If all of this seems a bit too onerous, particularly as you begin cultivating more than one mentor (formally and informally), think about the payoff. The guidance you get from a good mentor will serve you well now and further along in your career. Early on, following soft-skills advice will help you appear more mature and professional and be deemed a problem-solver or team player. For many young professionals whose smarts and technical skills are obvious, these intangibles will set you apart and put you at the top of the promotion list.

A good mentor can also help you organize your thoughts, reconsider your assumptions, and offer an alternative view or alternative ideas for how to get things done or to make progress. A mentor can also help you reflect on your career and your life without the worries about how what you say— perhaps about work-life balance or questions about whether you are in the right career—will impact your job or relationship with your boss.

What's more, if you take the time to develop a relationship with a mentor and it becomes a fluid, easy relationship, that mentor is more likely to remain a go-to source later in your career when you need advice or face even more difficult decisions or workplace issues. A more senior professional in your field who knows your professional history and development and has had a unique look at your career, your weaknesses, and your strengths can be a huge asset; this is someone who knows you well enough to go straight to the heart of a decision or situation to actually help you reach a solution.

Another big plus: your mentor has experience. Experience means contacts. A strong relationship means he's more likely to provide access to his network of professional contacts when it's time to look for your next job. Someone he knows is bound to be looking for someone like you to fill a job and you want and need access to that kind of referral, particularly early in your career.

Your mentor might also have a leadership role in your industry's key associations, which could mean a segue into junior leadership roles of your own when he's asked to recommend people for posts. Those small career boosters can have a big payoff down the road. Whatever the case, these contacts will serve to help you build up your own network. And it's not just a cliché: at critical points in your career, your success will largely depend on who you know.

BY THE END OF YOUR FIRST YEAR

Much of this section has focused not on technical skills and abilities, but on the nuances of learning the ropes of workplace norms, relationships, and practices, and on laying the foundations for getting ahead. Mastering your actual job during the first eight to twelve months is also critical—but you already knew that, right? As you near the end of your first year on the job, you should have established important relationships; gained and used a mentor or two; built a framework for working with your boss, peers, and senior staffers; and, yes, become highly proficient in your job function. Hopefully, you've also had the chance to explore—at least tangentially—other areas of the company and work on some projects or assignments outside your normal scope.

As your first year draws to a close, you should also have a strong sense of what you want to do next. What now? It's time to put that foundation to use to get promoted.

CHAPTER 5

GETTING TO THE NEXT RUNG OF THE LADDER

You've accomplished your first-year goals, maybe more, and now you're thinking about the next step up the ladder. Getting promoted in the first two years, particularly in companies where the norm is longer, is a sign that your career-building is going well. If you've reached the peak of the learning curve in your entry-level position, your boss or a mentor might already be floating the idea of a promotion or hinting at a juicy raise.

The people most likely to get promoted are those who have demonstrated excellence in their work and a good understanding of their group, its needs, and how what they do (or their department does) fits into the broader goals and profitability or growth of the company. What's more, they have usually developed the right relationships and shown that they can work with more than one personality type (i.e., they can get along just as well with the grumpy but technically brilliant senior staffer as with their more personable colleagues). Also key: evidence that you can handle more responsibility than you have (remember that project you volunteered to do analysis for last month or that research you picked up when a more-experienced colleague got the flu?).

Finally, the most likely to be promoted are those who do not view a promotion as something they're entitled to. Doing great work doesn't *entitle* you to a promotion or title change or even a raise. Rather, it qualifies you for one. Once you know you're qualified, you'll still likely have to make your case for a promotion, title change, or raise. But before you head into the boss's office to ask, there are a few things to consider, assess, and understand.

WHAT'S NEXT?

It's likely you've got a good idea about what you'd like your next step to be. Perhaps you want to emulate the analyst down the hall, whose promotion last year landed him a spot on a team you'd really like to work with. Or maybe your industry or firm has a more regimented path for moving up and it's clear that the next step is to take the word "junior" off of your current title and become a full-fledged associate. In some fields—the sciences chief among them—promotions aren't as important as increased responsibilities and/or raises that come with them.

The point is, as you suss out what's next, look around for clues about typical paths and timelines for moving up—if you haven't already. Don't just consider the immediate next step, but also where that position and title will take you one or two jobs later. If it's not where you want to be down the road—or you aren't sure—take the time to figure out if there are off-ramps to other paths or other next-step options that will get you where you ultimately want to be.

You should also find out whether your next intended move is one that is likely to forever pigeonhole you into a particular path or specialty. That's just fine if you're quite certain it's the one you want to take and you can see yourself moving up and forward at each step on that path. But if you're not so

INDUSTRIES WITH REGIMENTED PROMOTIONS

You could be the brightest young star on your team or find yourself assigned to tasks well above your pay grade, and *still* not land a promotion or significant (promotion-like) salary increase after a year or two. Some fields have well-known, if not codified, policies or norms about promotions that sometimes have little to do with how great your work is or how many accolades you receive from higher-ups (although, those things will help you get promoted on the early end of that rigid promotion timeline). While there are exceptions to every unwritten (or written) rule, here's a look at a few industries with more regimented promotion schedules:

Accounting. In general, at the Big Four firms (Ernst & Young, PricewaterhouseCoopers, KPMG, and Deloitte), if you are a new grad hired as an associate, it takes three years to become a senior associate. Usually that promotion is predicated on earning a CPA (which the companies typically pay for) and/or required designations (say, in tax accountancy), so it could be longer. In some cases or some divisions of these firms, a promotion could come in two years, but it's generally rare. Smaller accounting firms often have a less regimented promotion schedule and a promotion is based more on merit, but there are sometimes fewer opportunities for moving up, and getting to the second step on the ladder is still likely to take at least two years.

Consulting. In IT consulting, it generally takes two to three years to be promoted the first time, and another two to three years to get to the third rung, although raises can be high, with significant responsibilities added in between. At big consulting firms like Booz Allen Hamilton, McKinsey, Bain, and Boston Consulting Group, the standard time to first promotion is two years. These firms are also, to varying degrees, known for dismissing up to 25 percent of new-grad hires after two years (sometimes three, depending on the specialty). If you miss a promotion at about two years, it's time to look for a new job, fast.

Investment Banking. Your usual first stop is analyst, where you'll both work and get intense training for the first two years. At most big firms (such as

J.P. Morgan or Goldman Sachs), you'll be eligible for a promotion to associate after two to three years depending on how you perform and, many insiders say, how well you "manage up."

Engineering. Promotions are often—but not always—regimented and based partly on designations you earn. In civil engineering, for example, to get a promotion, most engineers must earn their Professional Engineer certificate. That can take five years. In other specialties or functions, like some in mechanical or biomedical engineering, you'd need certifications and an advanced degree to get promoted. Pursuing those can take two to four years.

certain you want to specialize or if you have concerns about the future job opportunities in that particular specialty, take a step back and reconsider your next move. Use the same logic to make sure you're not going in a career direction where jobs are on the decline. A lot of industries are structured like a pyramid; jobs are fairly plentiful at the entry-level and associate levels, but thin out considerably the closer you get to the top. If yours is one of them but even knowing this, you're certain it's the path you want, just know you're going to have to work extrahard to nab one of those coveted top spots.

If you're not exactly sure what the next best step might be, think further ahead. What kind of work do you want to be doing in five years? What title would you like to achieve in five years? What sort of responsibilities do you want to have in five years? Once you've answered these questions for yourself, work backward and figure out what position you need just prior to that five-year-out job and then to what slot you'd likely need to hold to get that job. This should be your next-step target on the career ladder.

If, however, you've got a good sense of where you want to go but there are several possible next steps to get you there, make an appointment to talk out the possible scenarios with your mentor. He might have some additional insight on how much potential one path has versus another, or which will put you in a position to work within groups where your personal and professional style and skills will be a strong fit. Mentors might also urge you to think outside your current list of would-be steps or even present options you hadn't thought about, like the value of making what might seem like a lateral move to get into a part of the company that's going through a growth spurt or that is more cutting edge.

What's more, your mentors—particularly informal mentors—can often give you an honest assessment of your chances of landing the next-step position you really want and can steer you away from, say, bad bosses or departments whose young professionals languish or get little development. As you build your career, you'll quickly realize that working for and with people who are smart, fair, generally pleasant to be around (even if the office environment is competitive, there aren't many professionals who truly want to work with jerks, yellers, or super-sharp-elbowed people), and who have a reputation for being good to work with will improve your quality of life.

THE POLITICS OF PROMOTIONS

Let's say now you know you're qualified for a promotion and you've got a strong idea of what you'd like to do next. Here's the good news: sometimes you won't even have to ask or bring up the idea. A growing number of companies are strengthening their focus on retaining young workers (both to reduce turnover and to develop talent who can fill the pipeline as older workers retire or scale back), and increasingly they are realizing that the best way to keep young talent challenged and happy is to promote. Granted, you aren't about to be skyrocketed to the top ranks, but as those above you move up, their positions need to be filled, and more and more companies are choosing to staff these positions from within.

Now for the less-comfortable news: in almost all work environments, politics of some kind or another play a key—sometimes significant—role in *who* gets promoted. Office politics are tricky to maneuver; most new-grad hires won't be at a senior enough level to be fully immersed in the politics of big promotions (more good news). But their bosses and the boss's peers are (which can be good or bad news). Simply put, politics in promotions are the subjective things that you have no control over—they've got nothing to do with your work (mostly) and often little to do with your qualifications.

Politics of promotion could include how well your boss likes or gets along with you, how well liked *your boss* is around the firm, or even which department has more pull than the others. While you can't completely change your boss—or your department's status—you can do a few things to win at promotion politics, without having to step into the murky (and mucked-up) political issues yourself. That's because when it comes time to climb the ladder, there are ways to transcend politics and help you stand out.

BE A RELIABLE PROBLEM-SOLVER WHO MAKES THE BOSS LOOK GOOD

If you complete assignments on time or early, step up to offer solutions to problems that arise in your work or around the office, and are generally seen as dependable and motivated, you'll stand out whether your boss has clout or not. And if he does have clout around the company or division, he'll be able to argue for more wiggle room to promote people.

If you're the young employee whom he relies on to take charge and rarely has to worry about, your name will be top-of-mind. On top of this, if your work is also excellent, you make him or her look good. Bosses like to promote and champion people who make their jobs easier and help them stand out (after all, they want promotions and raises, too). At the end of the day, it's those folks who are a boost to his reputation, too.

BE AN (UNDERSTATED) LEADER

Have your peers begun coming to you for advice? Does the boss or a senior colleague look to you first when something needs to be done—and done right the first time? When you volunteer to take on extra work or help out in another group or department, do you resist the urge to boast loudly about it but quietly let people know? When the most recent natural disaster struck halfway across the world, did you e-mail HR several times to push for the company to offer?

These are all examples of understated leadership. Taking on responsibility for orphaned projects and tastefully touting the results (or just the fact that you took on something everyone else ran from), offering to help peers or colleagues with simple skills they might be weak in (say, formatting Excel perfectly), or speaking up respectfully after you've floated an idea with a mentor if you have a solid idea for improving what your team does, also add to your reputation as someone with leadership potential. Doing these things with a positive attitude and without acting like a savior or demanding praise is important, too.

CONSIDER THE SMALL STUFF

Little things can play into the politics of perception. Again, it can be hard to do much about the perception of your boss or others in your group, but you can do some things to avoid any hint of negative perception around how you work or your personal values in the workplace. The less ammunition you give a supervisor (or his peer vying to get his people promoted or give his junior employees big raises from a small pool) to use perception against you, the better.

That means you should avoid a few things—and excel at a few others. Avoid office gossip, but not with your head in the sand; most gossip does have some grain of truth or at least contains a valuable bit of information, so don't completely ignore it, but make sure you're not the one spreading it.

Try not to discuss actual politics. You might be a staunch Republican but the person signing off on your promotion might not be. Avoid going overboard discussing your personal causes or outside activities. You want to be friendly and personable, but you don't want to seem fanatical or end up oversharing about an outside activity that might be frowned upon by even a select few.

Excel in how you present yourself. Speak clearly, dress professionally, and prove your commitment (that stay-a-little-later-and-arrive-a-little-earlier theory applies here).

And perhaps the most important—and understated—spot to do particularly well: communication. That includes writing, something many managers complain that young people (and yes, older professionals, too) don't do all that well. In fact, a number of firms are bringing on writing instructors to coach employees on communicating more clearly and succinctly. If your company offers it, take advantage. And all communication—e-mails you send to the boss and others, memos and proposals you handle, communications with peers—should be professional, logical, grammatically correct, and well structured.

THE SUBTLETIES OF MOVING UP

Finally, you need to understand the subtleties of how people move up in the firm and try to work within those confines. The key is to look around and take stock of how those people who get promoted do it and try to work within those norms.

If newbies are promoted lockstep, after a certain number of years, certain certifications, or other measurable achievements, don't push to move up just because you're good at the less-tangible or more-political elements of promotion-getting. Or if it's an unwritten—or even unspoken—rule that staffers have to do the work of the next title up for a time before actually being promoted, don't go to the boss a week after you get some of that responsibility and demand (even nicely) that you get the title and pay to go with it. After all, if this is the culture of your firm, the very fact that you're being given that work is a sign that you're close to a promotion, so don't blow it. On the other hand, if the only people who get promoted are those who ask—and show proof of their accomplishments to the boss—by all means, gather your evidence and get ready to ask.

Getting Your Mentor Involved

If you've developed a strong relationship with an informal mentor, it's possible she can help with the political minefield you might be facing. For starters, she can clue you in to the culture of promotion at the firm. And she can coach you in how to push without being annoying and point out areas you might want to highlight to get promoted (for example, a mentor a few levels up might know where the big growth will be next year before it's announced and could help you make a case that would put you at the front of the line to be a part of that growth area). Beyond that, she could put in a positive word for you, or plant the idea of a promotion in the mind of your boss if she's in a position to do so (and if it will help your cause).

With a formal mentor, your chances of wading out of the politics and into a promotion are already better. A study by Gartner Group showed that 25 percent of people who enrolled in a company's formal mentoring program had a salary-grade change in the five-year period they studied; only 5 percent of people who didn't enroll had a change in salary grade. What's more, the study found mentees were promoted five times more often than those not in a mentoring program.

If you're taking part in a formal mentoring program, the

company is probably looking for feedback about your growth and development. But they're also looking for the same sort of feedback from a whole host of mentors about many bright young employees at the firm. So it's critical to be clear with your mentor about your promotion goals and if you've developed a good relationship and your mentor is a fan of your work, you can ask him to speak up or send a note on your behalf. Often your mentor's clout will be enough to offset the rest of the politics of promotion.

FILLING IN THE GAPS TO GET PROMOTED

As you do your "what's next" analysis and consult with your mentors and trusted colleagues, scanning the lay of the land on promotion structure, you might find that you need to develop a critical skill or compensate for a weakness before you stand a chance of moving up. It can be frustrating, particularly if you're used to being praised and advancing in most things you do, to discover that even with a laundry list of accomplishments, one thing—you might even consider it a small thing—is holding you back from moving up or getting that title that will earn the respect you need to really accelerate your career. So, get frustrated, get mad, get indignant— let yourself feel those things for a short time. Just don't stay in that frustrated place for long (a few days, a week at most). Then develop a plan to get what you need in order to move up. Here's how.

WHEN YOU NEED TO BUILD A HARD SKILL

A hard-skills gap is the easiest to overcome. Once you know where you need to develop, you can do so in a few different ways. For starters, look to see if your company offers any internal courses or online tutorials. If they do, take advantage of these. You can also search for external courses (your company might reimburse you). In many cases, online tutorials or courses will come with or link to practice tests or skills quizzes.

As you get comfortable with the new skill, you can—and should—look for opportunities to apply your growing knowledge in real work. If getting practice is an issue, as you become more proficient, volunteer to handle such work on the next project that comes your way or ask a senior staffer if he needs a hand with such work. If it's someone you'd consider an informal mentor—or a trusted colleague—you might even explain that you really need the practice to prove you've mastered this skill; provide evidence to show you have gained experience so there's no worry that you might screw it up. A formal mentor can also help you identify opportunities to show you've made progress.

You can also seek out a senior colleague or a peer who is a whiz where you're weak and ask for help. If you can, offer to help him or her with something he needs a boost with. Peer-to-peer learning like this often sticks faster and can be less intimidating.

Also key: make sure the boss knows about your pursuit and progress. Be proactive and tell your supervisor that you've recognized a weak spot and have started a class or begun to sit with the office whiz to shore up the gap. Send periodic updates about your progress. And once you've got something to show for your efforts—be it results of that work a senior staffer let you handle, or a top grade in a course—make sure the boss knows. If you haven't been able to find assignments that will show what you now know, this is the time to ask for something that can help you prove you've progressed.

Why does the boss need to know? Above all, because taking responsibility for a skills deficiency shows a high level of maturity and self-reflection. What's more, it shows you are committed to improving your work and contributing to the firm. That can be a powerful thought to leave with your supervisor when opportunities to move up arise.

When You Need to Build a Soft Skill

Soft skills can include anything from relationship-building and communicating to adaptability, ability to take criticism, critical thinking or decision making, active listening, and teamwork. Admittedly, building soft skills can be harder because it's simply harder to describe and understand what it takes to develop them. Making it tougher, when a supervisor or colleague says you need to work on taking criticism better or listening in a more active way, he often offers less description and fewer details about what he means than he would when telling you that your grammar in proposals needs work.

Soft skills can, by their nature, be vague and an ideal can be difficult to describe—and your mastery of them can be subjective, to boot. What's more, there's not really a class you can take or a typical tutoring scenario you can take to improve them. That means improving will take more work on your part.

The first thing you need to do? Assess how big the issue is. If you've been told to work on, say, taking criticism better (and putting it to use) in the past and have been actively trying to improve, you might not be able to tell if you've improved enough. To get a clear picture of your progress, meet with those who gave the feedback before and anyone who has been helping you improve. Ask each of them to honestly assess your progress. In many cases, if you have made an effort and have been working with a mentor, you might be doing better than you first thought.

Some people find these things come naturally. But if you've got room for improvement, practice really does make a difference. First, get as many details and specifics as you can. Ask your boss, colleagues, or mentors for specific examples and scenarios where your soft-skill deficit has been apparent. Take notes on what you hear and listen for the actions they associate with your soft-skill deficit. The skill itself, like "focus" or "sociability," might be hard to define, but the

QUICK FIXES FOR SOFT-SKILLS GAPS

Because soft skills can be so hard to describe—and yet can be so important in getting ahead—mastering certain ones is key. Here are four of the soft skills that bosses most frequently cite as necessary, and some tips on how to prove you've got them.

Adaptability. Simply put, people who are adaptable can adjust their own behavior and style to work more effectively when they find themselves in a new or changing situation, when they suddenly have new information or too little information, or when they're thrown into an unfamiliar environment or group. To improve your adaptability quotient, you first need to recognize that you must be able to switch gears and process information more quickly—that is, recognize situations where you are most likely to be rigid or resist change. Then, keep an eye out for such a situation to arise and stop yourself. Try to focus on flexibility—not on the big, bad change as a whole. Often, people who become rigid or bristle at change are worried about the worst-case scenario . . . thoughts like all your work is worthless now or the deadline will never be met. Instead of going from zero to worst in a split second, focus on figuring out several outcomes. "I might need to redo some of my work, but if I do X and Y, I should still manage to meet the deadline and use that other analysis for something else later on."

The key is to pause, take a breath, and don't get caught up in the "this isn't how it was supposed to be" thinking. Another big help: transform yourself into a little Mary Sunshine when you *most* want to stand firm. Inside, you might be feeling pressure and worry about doing a proposal with a new group or reworking the format for a presentation to one you've never done before. But your words are, "Sure, no problem. We'll figure it out." With a smile. Psychology studies show that, often, simply smiling and forcing out a few positive words can relieve anxiety. At the least, you'll appear more adaptable and, as they say, fake it until you make it.

Critical Thinking. Everyone wants it in their employees; not everyone can explain it. Thinking critically is part intellectual, part conceptual, part analytical, and a whole lot of applying and synthesizing information. In short, you take what you know, what you don't know, assumptions from your experiences, your observations, and information you've gathered for, say, a proposal or a report, and evaluate how each disparate piece of information comes together or impacts the others—and try to connect the dots to come up with a solid guide or set of answers or solutions. Often, you'll need to apply critical thinking to a question or problem. Just being smart isn't enough. And just Googling for answers is really not enough. You have to be able to sort out all you know and all you don't know and come to some conclusions—and present them clearly. This can be difficult to learn if you aren't practiced, particularly because critical thinking is very self-directed and requires the ability to correct and rethink your own thoughts, too.

To get into the practice of critical thinking, it helps to go through a checklist of sorts when you consider information. When you get information, ask yourself what else you need to know, what questions this information answers, what problem it presents, how you can interpret it in various ways, how this information relates to what you already know. As you do this, take notes on key findings for each bit of thought and information. It could help to draw out the relationships you find—literally—making your central idea or would-be conclusion like the center of a spiderweb. As you add rings and links to outer parts of the web, see where those links fall apart or disconnect. That's where you rethink—is it okay that this doesn't connect to that, or do I need to reassess? Another helpful idea: consider what you know, believe, and have learned as a connect-the-dots puzzle where the answer or solution you want to present or discuss is the picture. What does that picture look like? Where does it lead? Is there an odd corner you need to reconsider? Critical thinking takes practice, so be diligent.

Active Listening. We all listen—or so we think. But do we hear what's being said? Active listening involves making a purposeful effort to not just hear the words a person says to you but also to try to understand the meaning and the entire message in those words. That means you've got to pay attention closely. By listening carefully—not just to hear but to glean vital details in the information and tone, you will be able to improve your work and your ability to influence people. You'll also go a long way to avoid misunderstandings, which is key to success on the job.

To improve your listening—rather, hearing—skills, when you're having an important conversation with a boss, peer, or client, try to shut out outside distractions, for starters. Block out the noise, thoughts of the next meeting, or the looming deadline. More important, block out your own voice. Often, we're forming counter-arguments or our own next thought—the thing we'll say as soon as this guy stops talking. It's absolutely impossible to listen carefully when the only person you hear in your head is you. Another key: stay focused, even if what you hear isn't all that interesting. If you find any of this difficult, try repeating the other person's words in your head as they are said. This can both help the message sink in and keep you focused. Acknowledge what you are hearing and occasionally ask clarifying questions—especially when you don't understand. Many work mistakes stem from thinking you probably understood what the boss said only to later realize you were off the mark and a simple question could have remedied that.

Team Orientation. Ah, in a workplace where individual accomplishments make headlines, being a team player might sound overrated. But it's important. If you are disliked around the office because of your sharp elbows or inability to get your piece of a project done in coordination with other team members, it will likely slow your move up the career ladder. Being a team player has much to do with how you interact with people in your group, on an assigned team, across divisions, and even with your boss. It often requires you to set aside your ego and pitch in where you are strongest and allow someone else to take the lead in an area where you aren't as strong.

The key to improving your team skills is to listen to others, consider the ideas and work they present, and honestly assess them against your own ideas and work. Also important: show your commitment to the team—don't miss deadlines, be willing to pitch in if someone in your group or on a project is having difficulty, and be prepared for meetings—otherwise, you're sending the message that your time matters more than theirs. You should also take time to learn a little about each person's job so you can pitch in (and prove yourself indispensable to the boss). Finally, share praise with people—whether they were directly involved or simply led you to that one piece of information that made your work sing.

action associated with it (say, looking off into the distance instead of making eye contact or going back to your desk to work on your piece of a project rather than joining teammates in a break-out room more regularly) isn't.

If you know the action, you can monitor yourself and take steps to change it—like focusing on a speaker by telling yourself to look up every few minutes or joining that team meeting even if you think you'd be better off working on your own. If you treat the soft skill as tangible by focusing on the *action* people associate with it, you can often master the skill through awareness and practice. The practice will make your improved reaction a habit. This will be useful not just as you climb the first rungs of the career ladder but for decades to come.

When You Need to Fix a Problem

If you've made a misstep at work—and trust me, you're bound to do it more than once in your career, no matter how successful you are—how you react and handle the problem is often more important than the mistake you've made. Let's say you've been humming along and doing well when suddenly, just before you were going to talk to the boss about applying for that post you heard about or asking for a raise, you discover you've flubbed an analysis or misquoted a price to a client or clashed with a colleague publicly. What do to?

Remain calm. People typically have two reactions when they make a mistake at work. They either feel horrible about screwing up or they blame somebody else. Here's a hint: don't do either. You can feel bad, but not to the point that you end up overstating the problem and making it worse. Whatever you do, don't pretend you didn't make a mistake or hope it won't be found out by the boss. Instead, go talk to your boss—now. It's better for him to hear it from you (even if you think that he'll never hear about the tiff you had in the hall, it's likely someone will tell him) rather than find out about it from someone else.

You should plainly state what happened and suggest a solution—or if you aren't sure what to do to correct the problem, tell him you take full responsibility for fixing the problem and ask him to help you come up with a solution and throw out a reasonable idea to start. Don't be shocked if the boss is a little angry at first. Mistakes cause problems, after all. But proactively admitting to and trying to fix a problem will pay dividends in the days and weeks to come.

What if your error or mistake happened because someone else fell down on the job? Again, don't cast blame at the start. Take the same approach you would if the mistake was your fault, explaining what you believe the mistake stemmed from and offering up a solution. Let's say the mistake stemmed from some incorrect information you were given. It's likely the boss will ask who gave the information. You should be honest, but not attach blame. Simply answer the question directly. The boss can—and will—suss out the root of any systemic issues.

If you've made a faux pas of a more social variety (that tiff with a colleague), apologize for a lack of maturity and explain how you'll handle a disagreement in the future—don't get into who's fault it was or who started the disagreement. You should also apologize to the person you had the run-in with. If you're not sorry for disagreeing, apologize for bringing the disagreement out in the open and suggest a way to solve your differences privately in the future.

At the end of the day, a one-time mistake or problem is easily overcome if you deal with it head-on. People will notice your effort to correct the issue and—because it's much more common for people to stew, complain, or blame—be impressed that you handled it right away and moved on. Let a mistake or problem fester or pretend it didn't happen, and your reputation can be damaged when the mistake is found, or when a colleague starts to shun you and others notice. This is a surefire way to kill your chances of getting that promotion.

PRESENTING YOUR CASE FOR A PROMOTION

In a company that doesn't map out promotions or doesn't have a "don't ask us, we'll ask you" mentality about moving up, you'll likely need to broach the subject of a promotion yourself. Again, observing the cultural norms of your office and company and getting advice from mentors and colleagues a level or two above you are key before you make a move. Once you have a good sense of how things generally work, you should gather your evidence into talking points you can refer to or use as an internal checklist when you begin to talk to people about real opportunities to move up. That list should include key accomplishments, new skills you've gained, training you've completed, traits that make you a good fit for the next positions, and some sort of proof of your aptitude for the type of position you are seeking.

Your key accomplishments will be critical and you should be able to cite specifics, like how your team and boss told you that the work on a key client proposal, which included an analysis of growth areas the company hadn't considered, was a big reason the company signed on. Then be able to quickly explain what was unique or outstanding about that analysis. Even better, if you have bottom-line numbers to add to your accomplishments list, you'll be able to quantify your value (yes, that sounds pretty soulless, but business is business). If you handled tasks or work typically reserved for someone with more experience, add that to your talking-points list (with specifics, of course).

As for aptitude and traits that make you a good fit for a particular step up, you want to have proof: concrete points to show that you're up for the slot you're interested in. If you want to take more of a junior leadership role, be ready to cite instances where you took ownership over something that several people worked on or where you served as lead for part of a project. You can also point to company-related volunteer positions or efforts you pushed through (like that push to get the firm to match donations for disaster relief). If you've received praise for your critical-thinking skills and your get-to-it attitude, for example, those are traits that you should note where it makes sense.

Once you've got these talking points down, there are a few ways to scope out opportunities and present your case. For starters, mentors can be a great conduit to a promotion—without a lot of upfront work on your part (sorry, you still need your proof points). A recommendation, or even a mention of your name in relation to an opening, from a senior, respected person can speed up the process and push you to the front of the pack for a slot. Make sure you let your mentor know when you identify a spot you really want. If your relationship is strong, you can ask a mentor to recommend you outright. Otherwise, be clear about your target position and wait for your mentor to make a next move or suggest how he might help.

Here are other approaches to consider. Based on the corporate culture and norms at your firm, one of these—or a combination of them—will be a good way to make your next-job target known and to present your case for a promotion or new position.

The Informal Approach

Many times, a low-key approach works if you've already been noticed for your work and potential in the company, particularly if you have had the chance to work with other groups or departments or on cross-group projects. As you narrow down the groups or positions you're most excited about, identify people you could approach in an informal way to get more information—be it about the group, department, or actual jobs available. You can also ask a mentor to put you in touch with someone in a group you'd like to learn more about.

The first people to approach are those you've had some contact with, even if it's limited. That might be more senior colleagues whom you interacted with on a project or peers you've met in passing but don't regularly interact with. The point is, they know your name or will quickly recall it and won't be puzzled by an e-mail or hallway chat requesting a few minutes of their time. When you ask to meet, remind the person how you know each other and state that you're starting to think about what's next for you at the firm and hoped to get some insight from a few people, informally.

If you don't think it's prudent for your boss to find out about your conversations, you can add a line mentioning you'd prefer to have these informal chats *before* you approach your boss officially about your next move. Most people understand what that means, so you won't need to belabor the point. Then ask if they have a few minutes—over coffee, lunch, or in their office—to chat about what it's like to work in the group or what opportunities might be coming up.

When you meet, start with a brief explanation of why you're there. That introduction should include a few sentences about what you've been doing (remember, those accomplishments and traits) and what you've been thinking about doing next. Follow that with a sentence or two about how those things led you to this department, group, type of work, and the conversation you're about to have. You'd like to get a feel for the opportunities and where someone like you might fit in.

Then, do a bit more listening than talking. Remember, this is informal, kind of like a fact-finding mission. The exception: if the person you're speaking to mentions specific positions that are open or coming up—and you instantly get excited—probe further for information about what the bosses are looking for in a strong candidate and, if the conversation is flowing easily, ask about whether you might be a good person for the slot. Before you go further—like asking for an introduction to the manager making the decisions—make sure you speak to your boss. No boss likes to hear that his staffer is after a job in another group from someone other than that person.

In most cases, the informal approach is just a starting point. You'll get a good deal of information about what's out there and you'll make contacts and—hopefully—make a good impression. The person on the other side of the desk will remember your name and your interest when it comes time to fill next-level slots. And in the meantime, you'll have made a more formal play for a promotion or move. Read on.

HUMAN RESOURCES AS ALLY

In some cases, you can move up to the next rung on the ladder while essentially staying in the same position—only with a higher title and more responsibilities. But in other cases, moving up may require you to leave your current spot and apply for another, higher, spot in the company. At some companies, internal job postings are the first official way to hear about a job—even if you've heard rumblings about an opening around the office. And company policies often require would-be candidates, even current employees, to apply formally. In most cases, you'll be required to tell your boss before applying and, frankly, your supervisor should be the first to know about your plans to apply for a post before you start filling out the online application form.

That said, human resources can be a good place to start when you're gearing up to apply for a higher position. If you hear about an opening, or see a posting on the company website, contact an HR representative informally. A good HR staffer will be able to give you critical insight into what type of person would be a good fit for a specific group and position. And in some cases, HR can help you make connections or keep you informed of company policies about internal applications.

At companies where HR has a significant role in career planning, your on-the-ground contacts are still important, but you'd be wise to use the HR avenues, too. Schedule a meeting with your designated career guide in HR and go over your thought process, your interests, and any specific positions you're excited about. You can tick off your accomplishments and traits. At the least, the HR rep will be able to guide you through any formal or informal corporate policies and point out possible pitfalls. He might also be able to point to positions you might not have known about or considered before. And when you *do* make a formal application, and HR screens the candidates, you'll be top-of-mind (and more likely to be top-of-pile) as he sorts through the people he'll send along to the hiring managers.

ASKING THE BOSS

If you want a promotion, eventually you're going to have to approach your boss. Again, depending on the culture at your company, he or she might very well be your first stop—before you reach out informally to others or to HR.

Since you've already had formal and informal reviews and been able to show your worth to your boss, she should have a good idea about what you want to do next, and the conversation won't come as a surprise. A really good boss will be on the lookout for move-up opportunities for high-potential employees. But even five-star bosses have multiple competing priorities and often can't devote as much time to career planning and development for staffers as they'd like. So it's important to make sure your supervisor knows exactly what you'd like to do next and has a chance to hear your accomplishments and your case for a step up.

With your interests and next-step targets in mind, ask the boss if she can carve out some time to discuss your career aspirations. Don't be vague about why you're requesting the meeting. You want your boss to know what's coming so she can think about it, too—and not stammer over your request.

How formal your conversation is depends on your relationship with your boss, but no matter what, you want to be clear about why you think you're ready for a new challenge or

A FEW THINGS TO KEEP IN MIND

Before you ask the boss to chat, make sure you consider the following:

- **Reality.** Is the company or department in a position—money-wise and growth-wise—to give you the promotion you want? If not, temper your approach with a dose of realism. State your case but explain you understand a move up might not be possible now.

- **Your Standing.** Remember, you don't deserve a promotion, you're qualified for one. If you're not confident that the boss would agree that you've got what it takes to move up, don't ask yet.

- **Protocol.** If you've been really shining in your position, you might think your performance warrants skipping the usual protocol. In rare cases, you might be right, but you should never make this assumption. You need to go through the regular channels unless told otherwise.

- **Company Needs.** You might need more money or a new challenge. But your case for a promotion shouldn't revolve around what *you* need, it should revolve around what the *company* needs—and how you can contribute to that.

- **Timing.** You want the boss to be in a good mood—or at least the right frame of mind—when you approach him. That means the week quarterly numbers are due or a morning before a stressful meeting is not a good time to discuss a promotion.

- **Follow-up.** Be persistent, but don't be a pest. If the boss points out something you need to do before you can move up, check in with proof you've progressed. If a slot you want is about to come open in a few weeks, ask to chat again then. But don't make every interaction about your promotion.

promotion, the thought process that led you to the target positions you want to discuss, the ways you've exceeded expectations (think: accomplishments on overdrive), and any evidence that you'd be a good fit (skills and traits) for the slots you'd like to be considered for. You also want to reaffirm your commitment to the company and your motivation to do more and grow. Openly address any trouble spots in your past that you have mastered as more proof that you are motivated and ready to move up.

If you want to make a move to another department, explain why carefully; you don't want your boss to wonder why you don't want to move up within her group or to take it as a personal affront. Plausible explanations include a desire to learn about other parts of the company, a specific interest in a growing area of the firm, or a lack of opportunities to move up in your own group.

Once you have stated your goal, stop talking and listen carefully to the response you receive. If the boss is excited or enthusiastic about your goals, she'll probably offer to help you get where you want to be and the conversation will flow pretty naturally from there. If you sense hesitation, hone in on where it's coming from and address it. You might say you sense concern about X and want to make sure you understand why. Or you might ask a follow-up question about how to get where you want to go. This offers the boss a segue into any concerns or obstacles she sees.

Whatever the case, make sure you leave the meeting with a plan for next steps, the okay to meet with people who can help you gain entry to the slots you want, an offer to connect you with managers who have slots you'd be interested in, or a combination of these things. Don't expect to walk away with a promotion in hand or a promise of any kind. You're setting the stage for moving up, making your case, and stating your goals and interests. Once those are clear, it will be easier to go back to the boss when you want to apply for a specific job or contact HR or other managers about openings.

WHEN THE ANSWER IS NO

Uh-oh. The dreaded "no." Sometime in your career, you're going to hear it, and experts say it's more common to get that first no early on in your career. One reason: managers say Millennials frequently expect to move up too quickly—often because they fail to see opportunities that exist within the jobs they have, be it the chance to take on more or expand the scope of what they can do in their role. This phenomenon is well documented, but knowing it exists can help you rationalize and understand a "no" to get to a "yes" faster. First, stay calm and don't let yourself sink into a negative state of mind. It's natural to be upset for a day or two, but deal with the disappointment quickly; dwelling on it will make it harder to get what you want in the long run. Talk to a mentor, trusted colleague, or friend about what happened and resolve to move forward. Simply put, consider the "no" as another opportunity to figure out how to improve your odds of moving up.

Next, look for—and ask about—the reason your request was denied. What skills and/or experience were you lacking? What do you need to do to ready yourself for a move up? Then resolve to seek out those things or ask your boss (and later, your mentor) for the kinds of opportunities to get there. And take the time to consider whether your request was reasonable. If what you ask for is too far outside the norm, no matter how brilliant you are, it will be hard to get a "yes." In this case, ask the boss what the more reasonable next step might be.

If the negative response has less to do with overreaching and more to do with timing, try to get a sense of when you should broach the subject again. And ask if there are step-up assignments or projects you can work on in the meantime. You want to keep building your skills and your accomplishment talking points so that the next time you ask, you have an even stronger case—good timing or not.

If the problem is more systemic, say the company is stingy with promotions or has gradually become less interested in developing younger employees, it might be time to consider looking for a job outside the company. But even as you assess that, don't slack off or complain that you're being treated unfairly. It can be hard to remain dedicated and focused under such conditions, but you'll need to do so to have a shot at finding your next employer.

CHAPTER 6

CAREER BOOSTERS: SETTING YOURSELF APART

Even if you're a standout performer and are well on your way up the professional ladder, there are things you can do to accelerate your journey. Some could pay off quickly and others set the foundation for adding value later in your career. These career boosters aren't required, but they're often the hallmark of the ambitious careerist. Being ambitious doesn't have to mean being a climber or stepping on others to get ahead. It does mean being proactive and doing a variety of things to keep you on track, get you noticed, and put you in the right place at the right time when a great opportunity comes along.

As the pace of change and technology continues to move at what seems like warp speed, who you know, who knows you, and how well you find ways to boost your skills, profile, and network will ultimately make the difference between a long slog up the career ladder or a brisk climb, accented by a few unexpected jumps along the way. The key is to find different opportunities to grow, to meet people, to become known because you never know where—or when—your dream job will come along.

INDUSTRY AND PROFESSIONAL ASSOCIATIONS

Industry and professional associations are among the most underutilized career development tools there are. Many younger professionals eschew them as unnecessary and too pricey to join. Others dismiss them as being for old dinosaurs trying to learn the new ways of business that you're already practicing every day.

But most industry and professional associations are much, much more than that. They're critical for educating yourself, expanding your professional network, getting a glimpse of what goes on in other firms in the same space, keeping up with industry trends and happenings outside the narrow scope of your own work, and finding early opportunities for leadership roles. That makes the cost of entry—and yes, even the $75 for add-on networking breakfasts and $20 webinars—worthwhile. (Some associations offer discounted prices to recent grads and some companies will pay for your membership to a key association; check with HR.)

Of course, joining is one thing. But participating is where the real benefits lie. You should join young professional subgroups, attend events and mixers, and get involved in activities, if only to build a broader group of peers to compare your experiences. But don't just stick with the youngsters—you want to meet people who've been there and done that and whose experiences you can learn from, if only tangentially. One of the easiest ways to get involved is to join a committee within the association. It could be a group closely related to your job or, if you're looking for exposure to other functions, you could volunteer for a committee that's totally unrelated. If you work in financial analysis, for example, join the association marketing committee. When you explore something unfamiliar, you're more likely to be exposed to new people and concepts. Gradually, you can volunteer for multiple groups and consider taking on leadership positions on committees, maybe even lead the effort to put together annual conferences or one-off seminars.

You should also take advantage of any continuing education opportunities the association offers.

As more people get to know you, it's likely you'll be asked to assist on other efforts. Say no if you really don't have the time, but consider each meeting, seminar, or planning session to be an opportunity to meet new people with similar career interests. You would never meet these people otherwise and, trust me, one day you'll be glad you know so-and-so at the company you want to work for so badly. What's more, many people find critical outside mentors through their association dealings.

The more immediate payoff for you: more to add to your résumé; add your professional memberships, any committees you're on, and leadership roles. You should also include courses or continuing education you've done through the association. And if your participation has helped your company in any way—say showing that your firm is emerging as a leader in best practices in your specialty, thus boosting its reputation—make sure the boss knows about it.

VOLUNTEERISM

These days, more companies offer volunteer opportunity for staffers. Those that don't are becoming more and more open to backing the volunteer efforts of their employees, even on company time.[31] Sound a bit fishy? After all, that means they're essentially paying you for the volunteer work you're doing elsewhere. But actually there's plenty in it for the company. For starters, letting you take a few hours here and there to do some social good can enhance its reputation and its brand. A number of studies have shown that giving people time off for volunteer work also improves retention and recruiting. Not convinced? A 2008 study found that 76 percent of 1,071 U.S. adults surveyed said they consider the perk important, reports Cone Inc., a Boston-based brand-strategy and communications agency.

So what's in it for you? Career-wise, it's a chance to expand your network, meet people outside your comfort zone and outside your industry, try your hand at new roles or skills, and, sometimes, take on leadership roles or involve yourself in team-building efforts that you can present as evidence of your readiness for the management track. In some cases, the goodwill you bring to the company through your efforts will be something that's recognized by HR and even various executives (particularly those who champion the same or similar causes). What's more, having interests outside of work—especially those linked to a cause you believe in—can fulfill a need to do something you feel passionate about, filling a gap during times when you don't feel all that passionate about the work you might be doing at the office.

Another bonus to volunteering is that people you will add to your network through that vehicle will have something in common with you that often has little to do with the line of work you're in. Because you'll likely have values and interests in common they'll be more likely to take a more personal interest in you—and vice versa—which will mean they'll get to know your career aspirations and your character. That makes for a powerful referral down the road.

Volunteering also offers the chance to stretch your skills, much like joining a committee outside your main work function at an association does. Look for opportunities in a nonprofit to try your hand at new roles or to develop skills you think you'll need in your career—or that you just want to build for your own development. These are skills you can add to your résumé. Be sure to also include on your résumé any leadership roles you hold and any bottom-line responsibility or results you've achieved at the nonprofit. Reworking a charity's budget and finding enough savings to, say, sponsor additional scholarships or special events for needy kids isn't just a good deed; it shows you can slice and dice a budget and find ways to create money or opportunities without adding to costs. If a marketing effort you help direct draws in 20 per-

WORDS OF CAUTION

Not all volunteer work is created equal—at least not in terms of its value as a career booster. Here's what to keep in mind:

- It's rarely a good idea to volunteer simply to get noticed on the job. You probably won't follow through with your volunteer commitments and that's not exactly career boosting. Look for something you feel strongly about and want to commit some time to.

- Keep in mind that touting your work with causes associated with polarizing subjects or those that are highly political might do more harm than good. That doesn't mean you should avoid them, but you should be more thoughtful in how you present it to your employer or future employer.

- If your company allows you to volunteer during work hours, make sure your regular work is done or that someone will cover for you first. Except in rare cases—and with pre-approval—volunteer work shouldn't interfere with the work you're paid to do.

cent more donations or thirty new volunteers, that's worth touting as a bit of marketing prowess.

ALUMNI NETWORKS

In the past, joining your alma mater's alumni network meant signing up online and entering a sort of black-hole database. You might get the alumni magazine and a few e-mails about events or webinars—more so if you joined a local alumni club chapter—and you'd get oodles of information about re-unions and big fundraising efforts (don't worry, those are still a part of the deal, including those calls for donations). But, really, that wasn't all that much of a career advantage.

The true upside came only if you pushed and prodded and searched the alumni database, going out of your way to (sometimes awkwardly) reach out to an unsuspecting fellow alum.

While it's still true that you'll have to do some legwork to take full advantage of your alumni network, many alumni associations are offering considerably more to graduates these days. You can thank the recession and lengthy recovery of the late 2000s for that. More are offering regular expert seminars, meet-and-greets, continuing-education opportunities, and—key for many people—dedicated alumni career services and networking opportunities. Most also have a professionally managed LinkedIn and Facebook presence, at minimum. And some are offering formal mentoring programs, linking successful alums in a particular career or industry with younger alums who want to follow a similar path. (As you become one of those successful alums, don't forget to return the favor by participating in the kinds of programs you benefited from.)

All of this has made it easier and much more worthwhile to get involved and meet people who have one big thing in common—no, not the hefty tuition bill—an affinity for their alma mater and as a by-product, for fellow alums. A close relationship with your school could also pave the way for you to get involved with recruiting for your company. In many cases, companies bring young alums along to their alma mater when recruiting or making company presentations to reach potential interns or new hires (remember your days as an upperclassman at those job fairs and corporate meet-and-greets when it was the recent grads whose voice you most wanted to hear?). Being a part of these trips not only makes you an asset to your company, it gives you insight into a skill that's prized among managers: recruiting and assessing job candidates.

Some other big perks of alumni associations include continuing education opportunities and seminars—many held in cities with big alumni concentrations—and one-off events that almost always involve a networking hour. Both are a way to add to that all-important group of whom you know and who knows you, and most schools offer these in some form. Participating can boost your odds of finding your next employer—particularly if you take advantage of alumni association efforts to link alumni who have jobs to fill with alumni who are job-hunting. A number of schools have programs, largely online, that specifically advertise positions that a fellow alum's company or employer hopes to fill with another alum. In the past, those efforts had been aimed at entry-level jobs for current students but many schools have expanded the postings to include positions for more experienced hires.

SKILL-RELATED CLASSES AND CERTIFICATIONS

For some professionals, certain certifications are required, or at least expected, in order to get ahead. It's a given in those cases that you should go for these certifications, but you'll boost your profile and reputation in the office just a little bit more if you earn them on the early end of expectations and don't wait for someone to tell you to get started.

Are there other classes or certifications you should pursue, beyond the ones required or expected? It's true that some people question the value of taking extra courses or earning certifications that aren't expected—and the wrong class or an off-the-wall certification probably won't do you much good. But if you take a strategic approach to what you pursue and consider both the skills you may need later on in your career as well as the topics that interest you, there can be a big payoff.

Meanwhile, in many professions, optional certifications can be a big career-booster, partly because they signal a commitment to a career path or because they convey a deeper level of understanding. For example, insurance professionals might not be required to earn a risk management certification or a charter in property and casualty underwriting, but doing so can quickly boost everything from pay to promotion opportunities.

Not sure what the right optional certification might be? That's not surprising since there seem to be dozens in every topic or field. Of course, some are more valuable than others. Most of the time, you can eliminate certifications that aren't offered or endorsed by the primary or better-known industry or professional associations. You should also ask your mentors or senior colleagues which they'd suggest you get, or look at the certifications noted behind the name and title of someone you want to emulate, or someone whose job you hope to be in in a few years. Their certifications are a good indication of which ones are helpful in climbing the ladder. What's more, earning them gives you something in common with a higher-up who could be a key to building your career, or who might be someone you want to add as a mentor (asking the person about prep courses to consider or if they can give you a few tips for studying for the exam is a great way to break the ice).

Classes that shore up a skills gap that is keeping you from a promotion, for example, are almost always worthwhile. And so are courses—even short one-offs or online classes—that play to a specialized area in your field. That extra bit of knowledge means you could, say, offer to assist on a strategic initiative that requires that specialized knowledge at work. In many cases, if you can show that a class is valuable to your work, your employer will pick up all or part of the cost.

Something else to consider: more employers lament the fact that many employees (young and old) have mediocre writing and communication skills, so taking a business writing course can be a big background boost to your career now and later. You won't necessarily get the same immediate career boost of a course that fills a job-specific or specialized need, but this is a skill that will serve you better for life. Plus, evidence of your new knowledge—clearer writing, stronger proposals, and better memos—will be noticed (and appreciated).

Of course, taking a class just for the sake of personal interest is fine, too. Not everything you pursue has to be—or should be—career oriented. The curiosity and balance such pursuits display could play well at the office anyway; a special interest could help you make a personal connection with a boss or higher-up, land you a particular consulting assignment, or simply make you appear a more well-rounded candidate next time you apply for a promotion or new job.

SPEAK UP, BECOME AN EXPERT

Ever go to a conference or seminar and find yourself enthralled (or at least educated) by a speaker only to discover later that he's only a few years further into his career than you are? How, exactly, did this twenty-five- or twenty-six-year-old guy land a spot on the podium? While a few factors probably come into play (for example, whom you know and who knows you), putting yourself out there to share the expertise you've built is one of the biggest factors. Knowledge and expertise really is an equalizer—you don't need a decade of experience to be considered an expert if you've earned a key certification, regularly participate in your industry association, and have some specialized (or in-demand) knowledge that's cutting edge or simply sought after by others.

It's not likely that you'll be able to do this your first year out of college but it's certainly possible by your third year or fourth on a career path—if you've laid the groundwork first. Among that groundwork: certifications, participation in industry groups, networking with alumni and fellow association members, being a strong communicator, and staying up on current industry trends. Aha, these career-boosters really do build on each other!

As you dig deeper into your profession and meet more people—and, most critical, share what you know via networking events, LinkedIn groups, a professional blog, or Twitter—you're bound to interact with people who are responsible for

POLICY WATCH—KNOW YOUR CORPORATE LIMITS

Check your company's policy for how employees are expected to represent themselves before you agree to participate in a networking event. The same goes for planning to Tweet or blog as a representative of the company (some companies won't object to employees maintaining a professionally focused blog, but might not want you to overtly identify where you work—and certainly won't be thrilled if you criticize the firm). Use common sense when you post, even on a personal blog. And be sure any professional blog you maintain is just that—professional. Make sure you don't need approval to invite guest columns or blog posts—and if you do need permission, get it even if the process is a bit of a hassle (in tightly controlled companies, it might be).

putting together speaking events that a first-timer or budding expert would be perfect for, whether it's a career exploration panel for college students, a one-day industry seminar for interns, or an in-house lunchtime enrichment session for new hires. (Expect to be a little nervous the first time up; practice with a peer, mentor, or someone you know to be a good public speaker.)

When you prove your knowledge or speaking abilities in small ways, it's likely you'll be asked to add your expertise on larger platforms. That could mean a guest column or blog post for an industry or alumni association or a spot on an industry panel that draws a bigger crowd than the local chapter session you participated in last year. If speaking and blogging aren't your thing, don't worry—it's possible to become a go-to person in less personally public ways (like an article for your company newsletter or a write-up that your alma mater can distribute to students who want to be in the industry).

Helping Others

It might sound counterintuitive if you feel like you still need plenty of help yourself, but lending your expertise and guidance and setting yourself up as a go-to person (even if it's just to the latest crop of interns) is a critical reputation builder and can be a crucial point of reference if you want to become a manager. Take the time to help a new-grad hire learn the ropes in the office or assist a peer who might be struggling with something you're quite good at. If a colleague is grappling with how to best implement a new strategy and you can introduce him to someone from your industry group who has faced the same challenge already, do so. If you see an opportunity to mentor a younger employee or offer advice to a college senior looking to break into the field, remember how helpful it was to have someone do that for you. The goodwill you create will pay dividends in the future.

As you take the lead on projects or initiatives, pay extra attention to junior staffers assigned to work with you. Don't coddle them, of course. But when your success depends partly on their success, it's always in your best interest to figure out a way to push them along or over a hump. That twenty minutes extra you take to review and offer advice on how to improve a memo or to help a junior staffer rework an Excel sheet for sharper analysis will be time well spent. Plus, down the road when your name floats out as a potential management hire at a firm where that staffer now works, you'll be glad to be remembered as smart—and nice to work with.

Translating Career-Boosters for the Here and Now

So how do you let people know about all these career-boosting activities without seeming like a braggart or brownnoser— or conversely, underplaying your accomplishments and the value they add to the company? Part art, part science might be the best way to describe the right approach.

First, the easy part: your résumé. Granted, your résumé is primarily a tool for getting a new job. But it's also something you can use to introduce yourself to a manager in another group at work and it's often something you're asked to send along when you're involved in professional association activities or networking events. Keeping it up to date is important and at this point in your career—with only your first postgraduation employer, a couple of internships, and little worry about running too long—it's also easy.

Classes directly related to your line of work can be listed right below your college degree information under the education heading on your résumé (and that comes after your experience section). Certifications and licenses get their own section, typically below education. Meanwhile, professional memberships and committee positions, along with volunteer activities and speaking or expert engagements, can be grouped together under a heading like "Activities and Honors," a section you should already have from your first-job hunt résumé. If your volunteer work involves a leadership role or is closely related to your career (if you're a financial analyst and serve as treasurer or budget analyst for a nonprofit, for example) consider adding it under the "Experience" heading after your current job.

It takes a little extra savvy to advertise your accomplishments in the office. Sometimes, you can throw in a passing mention in natural conversation—for example, in response to a question like "Have any big weekend plans?," you might say, "I'm going tree planting with the environmental nonprofit I'm involved with," or "I need to do some homework for the Web design class I'm taking." Other times, that job-critical course you just finished might warrant a more formal conversation or note to the boss—i.e., "I just wanted to let you know that I've completed my accounting certification, so if there are any accounting-related projects you'd like me to take on, please let me know." In all likelihood, you'll have already told the boss about a class you take, particularly if he has to sign off on it for you to get reimbursed by the company. But that could have been months ago, so it's worth following up.

Just remember, you're detailing an accomplishment and you should make it clear what you think your new knowledge or skill means to the company (or to the assignments you can assist with going forward). But you shouldn't march in, transcript in hand, offering proof that you should now get that promotion you've been asking for.

By all means, keep trusted mentors informed of your accomplishments; the same goes for higher-ups you've had informal chats with as you've scoped out promotion opportunities. You can be more overt if the boss directed you to a certain certification or activity or if a senior staffer you admire was once involved in the same speaker series or blog (remember, building commonality is important on your way up the ladder; research shows that people are—for better or worse—more likely to hire and promote people they like and who are similar to them in key ways, including professional pursuits).

If you're nearing annual-review time, it's a good idea to write up a list of some of your extracurricular (but career-oriented) activities and to recap your progress in courses or certification work. It's also a time to casually mention how you've tried to be a resource to the new-grad hires who've come aboard in the last year.

CHAPTER 7

YOUR
NEXT JOB

So far you've come a long way in developing your professional career. But now you're maybe three or four years into your path, you've been promoted, and you're ready for more. Whether there's a roadblock that prevents you from doing that something more at the company you work for now or whether you simply want to work somewhere new, there's little expectation that an ambitious professional will spend her entire career at one company (or even two or three). Many successful professionals say moving up, finding new challenges, and, yes, getting paid better, often means going to a different company. Beginning to feel the same way? Consider yourself at the tipping point. This is typically when your next-job hunt begins.

A first job is a memorable experience. If you ask most people about their first job—even years later—they can probably recall a lot of details about what they did, what they valued, what they were glad to walk away from. Ask them about their second job, and their responses will probably be less specific. It's often a struggle to recall as many details about that stepping-stone job, the one that set the stage for the big job they landed after that.

While less memorable, your second job (and in this context, that means with your next employer) holds a lot more weight than many people realize. This is the job that can often set your career path—and your professional success—in motion.[32] While a first employer is often an entry into a field, a second employer—and the job you take there—is a signal to those around you (and future employers) about where you want to go. Landing the second job you want is a key indicator for all future employers that you've already impressed somebody—and more likely, several people—enough to have trumped the other whiz kids who applied for the same post. What's more, in a second job you have more opportunities to shine because you're no longer the new grad or the former intern (even if you've been at a firm for several years and have been promoted, it can be hard to shake that mantle sometimes) but the smart, great-fit new hire who accomplished so much at such-and-such company. You are, simply put, considered an experienced hire. Also important to remember: after your second job, in most fields it's far less important where you went to school; your professional experience and accomplishments will be significantly more important. Unless, that is, your second job doesn't deliver or advance your career in a real way.

To avoid this fate, you'll want to choose your next move carefully. The first thing to do is give some thought to where you want to work, what you want to do, and how it aligns with your broader career goals, what challenges you're looking for, whether you want to branch out or specialize, and what kind of environment you want to work in. You'll also need to think about—and plan—how you will present yourself. This will likely be your first full-fledged job hunt that's not assisted by a career services office. And this time, you've got more experienced competition to contend with—not just your peers and colleagues but other smart professionals in other careers looking to edge into a field. In this kind of competitive environment, your image, both online and off, is key.

PAGING THE IMAGE POLICE

Before you begin your full-fledged job search, start cleaning up your image (hopefully it just needs some dusting and not the heavy-duty bleach and scrub brush). Eliminate any questionable photos from social-networking profiles and ask your friends to un-tag you in any less-than-professional photos on their profiles. You should also remove any links or comments that might lead a recruiter to question your character or trustworthiness. Monitor comments made by friends on your personal page and, if needed, block their comments from being seen by outsiders. Recruiters often check, and even if your personal life and professional persona are very separate in your mind, they're one and the same to someone who doesn't know you.

A 2009 Careerbuilder.com survey of 2,600 hiring managers found that 35 percent of employers reported that they found content on social-networking sites that caused them not to hire a candidate. Some 53 percent cited the posting of provocative or inappropriate photographs or information as the reason, and 44 percent said posted content—photos, posts, or status updates—showing a candidate drinking or using drugs led to a person not being hired. [33]

If you have a personal blog, make sure your most recent posts—and any you write from now on—are free of political rhetoric, cursing, or other generally questionable or unprofessional comments. Also remove any negative comment about your employer, colleagues, or other firms. If you have a professional blog, make sure you link it from your social-network and LinkedIn profiles—better that you provide a link to click to than to have a potential employer randomly find one. If you don't have one, consider weaving professional posts into your personal blog or starting a separate professional blog.

Type your name into Google and other major search engines or aggregating people sites like Pipl.com. Then type your name and some identifying information (like your employer or an activity you're known to be involved in or even the fraternity you belonged to in college) and run the search again. And again. If you find something unflattering and you know the person who posted it (say the fraternity webmaster), ask nicely to have it removed. If you find more than a few things, you might want to consider using a service that can clean up your online reputation for you. Reputation Defender.com, Defendmyname.com, and Naymz.com are a few. These services could cost anywhere from about $30 for each item they help you remove to thousands of dollars for a more comprehensive sweep.

FIGURING OUT WHAT'S NEXT

Once you've made sure you're presenting a squeaky clean image to the world, it's time to tackle those crucial decisions like what kind of job you want, where to apply, and how what you do next will get you to the job after that. At this point in your career, you probably have a pretty good idea of what you'd like to do next. After all, you've spent plenty of time mulling it over internally, talking to people in your field, and discussing it with your mentors. Even more important, you know yourself better than anyone else out there—and that includes an understanding of what motivates and excites you in your work. Now, if you haven't already, you need to merge those things with career possibilities you've already scouted for a clearer picture of what kind of jobs will be right for your next step. An internal gut check (am I really qualified, do I have the skills for this, am I ready to move on and up in this capacity, do I have the personality for this?) and conversations with your most trusted mentors will help you narrow that list further. You can skip this step, but if you do, you'll probably find yourself applying more haphazardly and with less focus; and even if you get an interview, that lack of focus and clear direction will be apparent to your would-be employer.

If you're at a crossroads and your path could branch in more than one direction, think about which is more likely to make you want to get up and race to the office in the morning. If that's too vague for you, imagine what a typical day

TO GRAD SCHOOL—OR NOT TO GRAD SCHOOL?

This is the point in your career when many ambitious professionals wonder, should I go back to school? Instead of looking for my next job, should I get a master's degree, or a law degree, or an MBA instead? In some fields— particularly banking and consulting, and to a lesser extent product management—getting an MBA is often a must; some companies essentially design their postcollege job track to be one that is three or four years—and out. You might get promoted in that time and it's not an absolute require- ment that you return to school for an MBA, but your options may be more limited or simply narrowed. That said, some of these firms have gradually carved paths for talented young professionals to skip the extra schooling and instead encourage earning a CFA designation. It's practically as time-consuming, without the benefit of two years off to study for it.

Likewise, for some engineers, a career can grind to a halt without a master's degree. And engineers who want to become managers often re- turn to school to earn an MBA to round out their technical knowledge with management and leadership know-how.

Not sure whether an advanced degree is necessary? Step back and take note of whether the people whose positions you want to be in one day have an advanced degree (or high-profile designation like the CFA). If some do and some don't, try to figure out why—and whether those who got the degree really got a leg up in their career-building. Ask them how useful they found the degree to be, and find out the details about how and when they obtained it. Did they attend school full-time, take evening courses, or attend a weekend executive program (the upside to that is your company is likely to pay for some or all of such a program)? Were they at similar experi- ence levels as you've reached now or was it after five or six years in the field, or once they reached an even more senior level?

Once you've completed your fact-finding, figure out where your aspi- rations fit in the various profiles of people you admire. Then talk to senior colleagues and mentors about what might be right for you. And if you've got a good relationship with your boss, broach the subject with him, too.

Personal preference and work style also come into play when choosing that second employer. If you work better under pressure and with constant deadlines, it's probably safe to say that a job or path where things are slow moving and time is less precious isn't going to satisfy that need to always be on your toes (and in all likelihood, you won't perform as well in such a job, either). Or if you thrive working with other people, an office environment where teams operate in a dysfunctional way or where there's more emphasis on individual achievement might not be the best fit.

Granted, at some point in our careers, most of us will take jobs that are critical career-building blocks but not exactly best suited for our work style. Pushing through, adapting, and finding a way to succeed in such situations is akin to earning a career merit badge, and can build coping skills that will serve you well even in good situations. But you shouldn't knowingly walk into a job like this for a pivotal second move unless you have no other way to get where you really want to go on the career ladder.

To better your chances of landing the second job that will be not just a stepping-stone but a catapult in building your career, you'll need to tap your network, rethink your résumé, hone your interview techniques, and have a plan for job-hunting *while you're still employed*. Landing that second job will be infinitely more difficult if you've already parted ways with that first employer (and can be more difficult even as a student). So even if you feel like you can't stand to be in your current job a second longer, do yourself a favor and stick it out while you conduct your job search.

would be like in each of these positions. Consider what your daily tasks would be and how what you currently do—and the skills and traits you're best known for—would be utilized and expanded in each possible path. You're likely to be happiest and most successful taking the road that puts your best-honed skills to use, while still challenging you and leaving plenty of room for you to add to those skills and take more of a leading role. Consider which path will offer more opportunity and interesting assignments when you're ready to move up or around; it's smart to be choosier about your second employer. Part of determining the right next job is assessing a strong fit and finding a culture that challenges you while playing to your strengths and offering room for growth.

YOUR NEXT-JOB RÉSUMÉ AND COVER LETTER

The résumé you used to land your first job probably looked like many first-job résumés, listing, as it should, all your internships and college leadership roles. But now that you have a few years of experience, it's important to refine your résumé to emphasize accomplishments from your postcollege work. Even if you've kept your résumé updated as you added certifications or promotion details, before you embark on a full-fledged second-job search, go over it thoroughly. You're no longer being hired as a new grad, so your employer isn't going to be impressed by all your college achievements and awards. It's time to remove all but the most prestigious from your résumé, and you should avoid mentioning them in your cover letter. Otherwise, you risk appearing less experienced than you really are, and a potential employer is likely to question how valuable your full-time work has really been if you still highlight college accomplishments. It sounds kind of obvious, but career coaches and résumé experts say leaving them on is one of the biggest mistakes they see when they review résumés of young professionals. Remember that the best résumés are a tool for letting a potential employer know what you can do for their company.

So your résumé bullet points should demonstrate how you used your skills to solve problems and bring value at that first job.

If you have had bottom-line responsibility, that should be clear on your résumé—and, if directly applicable to a position you are applying for, in your cover letter, too. A cover letter from your first-job search might have discussed how you raised money for a school group or managed to whittle the budget for your sorority to save it $5,000 during the downturn. But that's not going to be compelling now and would likely be off-putting to a next-job recruiter. Instead, skip those college-related bottom-line boosters and highlight the fact that the analysis you completed saved your company $150,000 or how the marketing program you helped create was directly credited with increasing visibility or sales for a client by 10 percent in six months. If you aren't able to point to key accomplishments that are more meaningful than those from college, consider delaying your next-job hunt until you are.

Finally, look at the requirements for the types of jobs you are applying for and make sure you tailor some of your résumé's bullet points accordingly. For example, if you're trying to land a financial consulting role at a big international company, your bullet points should focus more on the financial consulting you've done for your firm's international clients than on other types of consulting you've done for its domestic clients. Don't skip the broader accomplishments, but be sure your résumé highlights the work that matters most to the next job you're trying to land.

Make sure your LinkedIn profile is also up to date and matches your résumé closely. Many recruiters and hiring managers do check for discrepancies. What's more, keeping your profile current increases the likelihood that your name will show up in recruiters' searches; big-name companies are increasingly directing recruiters to search LinkedIn *before* posting a job, and more independent retained recruiters are starting there, too. It's also smart to sharpen your executive summary on LinkedIn, particularly if it mainly lists your job duties or responsibilities. Replace this list with a directed statement about your accomplishments and strengths, similar to what you might write in a cover letter. While you're at it, if you have a profile on file with a professional or alumni association, be sure to update it.

Your Cover Letter

You should take a similar approach with your cover letter. Make sure it starts with a broad statement about, for example, the breadth of consulting work you've done. It should then focus in on how you developed a keen interest and expertise in financial consulting, as evidenced by X and Y results. Now, you might say, you want to focus your skills on digging deeper and doing the same with one company rather than spending a little bit of time with a number of firms. Of course, you'll also need to explain the value you think you can bring to the firm you're applying to and, if you have specific consulting work that mirrors what your target company needs, by all means, mention it in your cover letter.

Most of the time, you have about twenty to thirty seconds to capture the attention of the person reviewing your cover letter. Think about that—count to twenty. Not much time, right? That's why it's critical to make the top of your cover letter clear, concise, and packed with information that will make the hiring manager want to keep reading. Each one you write should be tailored to the job you are applying for. There's absolutely no need to waste space in the first paragraph explaining why you're writing when you're applying for a specific position (if you're seeking an informational meeting or interview, you can be less specific, but you should also try to have a mutual contact in your professional network make an introduction, first). Overall, your cover letter should be no more than three or four paragraphs and less than a page.

First paragraph. Right off the bat, you should mention two or three concrete things that make you a better choice for the job than everyone else who has applied—specific achievements, accomplishments, tangible evidence. End the first paragraph by clearly stating that you want to bring these skills and ability to deliver such results to the target firm; if you have a specific reason for wanting to work at that particular company—say, a deep admiration of their brand or a direct interest in an area that company is known for—you can mention that, too. You might say, "In every role I've held and on every business analysis I have completed, I have managed to find ways to save companies money without compromising quality or future business. My ability to quickly assess growth opportunities and work with teams around the firm to pursue those opportunities has been instrumental in increasing revenues for the company. I'd like to bring these skills and results to Big Widget, a company I've long admired for its agility and focus on quality and trying new things in the field."

Remember, the first paragraph should relate your prior accomplishments directly to the job you're seeking, so it's likely you'll have several first-paragraph versions as you apply for jobs at companies with slightly different focuses and needs—even if each of the positions essentially requires the same skill set. In this case, a similar job at another firm might require doing business analysis and implementation for, say, acquisitions as a way to grow. In that case, your first-paragraph example above should mention your success with acquisition analysis, or, if you don't have much, a desire to take those skills further outside the bubble of one firm.

If someone in your professional network is an employee at the firm and pointed you to the position, be sure to mention that in the first or second paragraph. It should not be the first sentence, but rather woven into your broader introduction and qualifications. You might say in a sentence at the end of this paragraph, "Joe Success, the division manager for Big Widget's Midwestern operations, pointed me to this position after we met when I was part of an outside consulting team working on an analysis of the division's expansion opportunities." If Joe is just someone in your professional network, you can say something like this: "It's partly because of these accomplishments that Joe Success recommended that I contact you." You don't have to detail how you know each other, although if there's a tangible professional link, it's worth mentioning. One exception to this end-of-paragraph placement: if Joe is already advo-cating your candidacy, you should be more direct and—with permission from him—copy Joe on the e-mail.

Second paragraph. You've hooked the hiring manager. Now it's time to back up your claims with more details about your professional and academic qualifications (no, not college classes, but any courses or certifications you've earned since then that are directly applicable). The idea is to flesh out the details of exactly how you will be able to offer the same or similar benefits to the target firm. This is also where you can draw in specifics from your résumé that would be useful in the position you want. Focus on your achievements, accomplish-ments, and results—not on your job duties. Those are impor-tant, but they don't tell much about what you've actually done. You should also try to relate your achievements to the specific requirements of the job, which you can glean from the job posting or description.

Third paragraph. Use this paragraph to more closely link yourself to the company. Show a clear relation—if the com-pany prizes brainy analysts who can also relate to people, you might say that you're exactly the kind of numbers wonk who can translate detailed analysis to managers and clients that you've seen succeed at the firm. Also in this paragraph, make sure to convey that you've done your homework and under-stand the company, its goals, and how the job you want fits into the bigger picture. If the company is aggressively work-ing to grow profits and grab market share from its competi-tors by developing cutting-edge or superior products and services and shedding less profitable products, you should mention why the idea of being a part of this excites you and how your experience can help achieve those goals in the job you're targeting. If you have a direct example of how you've done the same already, even on a smaller scale, cite it in this paragraph.

Last paragraph. This one should be short and sweet. Thank the reader for his or her consideration and make it clear that you are confident you are a great fit for the position and the company. Some experts recommend that you end by saying you will call or e-mail to follow up shortly. In more aggressive industries or companies, that might be okay, but for the most part, it's better to end by saying you look forward to speaking further about joining the firm (note, that's the more direct and confident way to say "I look forward to hearing from you"). You can still make that follow-up call in a week or so. End with your signature (with a pen and your name typed out underneath) and contact information.

Gut check. If you don't feel confident about the quality of your résumé or cover letter, seek advice. It can be tricky to get counsel from someone who currently works with you, even a mentor, unless the person knows you're looking for your next job. If this is the case, reach out to a trusted outside mentor, a more experienced friend of the family who is in the same field, or someone in your alumni network—or alumni career services if your alma mater offers it. If this isn't possible, consider a career coach who specializes in dealing with professionals in your field or industry.

IT'S WHO YOU KNOW, FOR REAL NOW

Here's a news flash: you're far more likely to land your next job—and the one after that and the one after that—with help from someone in your professional network. Mark S. Granovetter, a Stanford University sociologist, wrote in 1995 in his *Getting a Job: A Study of Contacts and Careers*, that "informal contacts" (people you aren't necessarily friends with but whom you know because of your work or another relationship you have in your life) account for almost 75 percent of all successful job searches.[34] Experts say that number has only risen as companies get pickier about whom they hire for key posts. That's partly because the well-documented but shadowy "hidden job market"—positions that are never advertised formally or are practically filled, via referrals or recruiter recommendations, by the time they are—makes up 50 percent to 75 percent of open professional positions.

However, having connections doesn't mean you can scrimp on your résumé revamp, write weak cover letters, or skip the online application forms most companies require. It *does* mean that your efforts are far less likely to end up in the HR black hole if you are able to make a direct—or even an indirect—contact with the manager who either oversees or is in charge of the early rounds of hiring for the position (that could be an HR specialist or a more junior manager charged with identifying the strongest candidates). A connection doesn't make you a shoo-in for the job, but it does get you on the radar screen and will most likely garner an interview. If the person who recommends you is an insider who has a lot of clout or sway with those doing the hiring, your résumé can go from the middle of the pile to the top in the time it takes to click Send.

How do you get this insider recommendation? First off, you need to be worth referring. Presuming you've been successful so far and are considered someone that others like to have on their team, you've probably got that covered. Next, you need to have a strong network—which includes everyone from your mentor to your peers, to contacts you've made through professional associations, alumni groups, and so on—that you've cultivated over time. If you've been savvy about keeping in fairly constant contact with a diverse range of people, you might not have to look that hard for a connection.

That's why it's so important to stay involved. If you've slacked off lately—say, skipping those professional association networking hours and losing touch with peers or mentors who've moved on—start reconnecting at least a few months before you get serious in your second-job search.

Otherwise, you risk looking like you've only reconnected because you need something, which isn't far from the truth.

But if you've kept yourself involved in all the ways described in previous chapters, you should have a strong network of people you can ask to refer or recommend you for a job. If you've done a really good job networking, you may not even have to ask outright for a referral for a job. If you plant the idea that you're open to moving on or that you're ready to find a new challenge even if it means leaving your current employer, you might be surprised to quickly hear a contact say they know of a job at their firm you might be a good fit for or offer to chat in more detail about what you might like to do next (which often naturally leads to a referral).

GETTING YOUR REFERENCES IN ORDER

When it comes to the second job, college or summer job references aren't going to cut it. It's generally okay to have one reference from a strong summer internship, but only if you've kept in touch with that person and he is up to date on your career progress and accomplishments. Don't wait until you're asked to provide references to figure out who to ask; by then you're likely a finalist for a job and a reference could make or break your chances. Instead, begin to suss out who will best help you make your case near the beginning of your job search. Keep in mind that the best references will come from people who support your work and your career and will show enthusiasm about your skills and abilities.

Whom to ask. A mentor who knows your work well can be a good reference. You will also need at least one recent or current supervisor. Consider tapping a first boss who championed your promotion or a supervisor who has since moved on to another role or company but whom you have kept in touch with at least occasionally. You can usually substitute a reference from a current boss with one from a senior colleague who has in-depth knowledge of your work and whom you trust to keep your job search quiet. If someone you've worked closely with now holds a management position at the company you want to work for, it's worthwhile to have that person as a reference, too (presuming you haven't already received a recommendation from the person to launch your candidacy).

How to ask. The experts at Quintessential Careers recommend an indirect approach, namely e-mail, which gives the potential recommender an easier way to decline. You don't just want a reference, you want a *good* reference, and putting someone on the spot is likely to elicit a yes, but not always a good reference. So, give the person an out, Quint Careers suggests, with an inquiry like this: "I'm beginning a quiet job search. Do you feel you know me well enough to provide a reference about my leadership/analysis/team-building/problem-solving skills?" If the person declines, don't get upset; it's a better alternative than a mediocre reference. If you're asking a mentor or someone you feel absolutely certain will have glowing things to say about you (say, that boss who pushed for your promotion and thinks you're great) you can be more direct and ask in-person or on the phone. However, if you sense any hesitation, think twice about using the person as a reference when the time comes.

What to do next. Once someone has agreed to serve as a reference, forward a copy of your current résumé and a link to your LinkedIn page. If needed, in a few e-mailed paragraphs update each person on your career progress since you last worked together. Occasionally update recommenders on the progress of your job search. Once you get to the point where you are a finalist and are asked to provide references or believe you will be, give your recommenders details about the job, the reasons you believe you are qualified, and a little background on why you want the job. If there's something critical you hope your references will get across, don't be afraid to offer a little guidance—just don't tell the person exactly what to say. For example, if the job requires leading a team, you might tell your references about that and say that the demands of the team leader are a more official brand of the informal role you often took on when you worked together.

Don't forget. Thank your recommenders and keep them up to date about whether you were offered the job they recommended you for and whether you accepted (if you declined, explain why). If you didn't get the job, you might want to ask your references if anything the interviewer asked them jumped out as a reason you were passed over.

If you find you need to be more direct, it's best not to ask outright for a referral. Instead, ask someone in your professional network, an alum from your alma mater, or a friend of the family who knows your work (and could be a conduit in your industry) if you can buy them a cup of coffee and get their advice or insights about your next career move, or inside information about the company they work for. Then make sure you stick to asking about just that. Do not, under any circumstances, ask for a job. And only, under rare circumstances—say, if your contact makes it clear they'd be happy to help you—ask the person to refer you or put you in touch with the hiring manager for a job you want at his company. You can ask your contact if she has time to take a look at your résumé and assess whether she thinks you'd be a good fit for the position. (Before you do, make sure, of course, that the conversation is going well.)

If you're connecting with someone you've interacted with before or see more regularly, you can often go a step further and ask for advice about how to stand out to hiring managers at his firm. End all of these conversations with a big thank-you and, if it makes sense, ask your contact if she has anyone else she'd recommend that you speak to as you suss out your next step or look to make a move. You can also ask the person to let you know if she hears of anything that might

GETTING LINKEDIN RECOMMENDATIONS

Since so many recruiters look to LinkedIn as a resource for finding candidates or for screening them after they've applied, recommendations from people you've worked for or with that appear on your LinkedIn profile can make your candidacy more viable than, say, someone who has no recommendations. But how, exactly, do you ask for one? Jason Alba, author of the book *I'm on LinkedIn, Now What* and a blog by the same name, offers this advice for securing a LinkedIn recommendation:

1. Write the contact an e-mail . . . don't use the "request recommendation" feature from LinkedIn. I think the e-mail is more personal.

2. Let them know you are working on your LinkedIn Profile, and you'd really appreciate a recommendation from them. You can even say, "it's like a letter of recommendation, only it should be about a paragraph."

3. With your brand in mind, coach them on what you want them to focus on. "I'd like to bring out X, Y, and Z. When we worked on that team together, I think you saw this in my work ethic (or whatever), and I'd appreciate it if you could write something to those points." Consider writing a paragraph as an example, and don't be surprised if they just copy and paste.

4. Make sure, in your e-mail, they understand this is not a relationship deal-breaker, and that if they don't, or can't, that's okay.

He adds: The job seeker who goes to his old boss, peers, or customers to ask for letters of recommendation is not begging; he's simply doing what he should be doing. . . . An approach like this is acceptable, and a chance to nurture a relationship.[35]

be a good fit for you. This gives her time to think about the impression you've made and about your qualifications, without being put on the spot. Many times, these conversations will naturally lead to tips about job openings, even if that doesn't happen right away.

A personal referral or note to a hiring manager is a long shot if the contact doesn't know you already (there's another reason it's important to maintain all those networking webs and connections) since it's his reputation on the line, too. But if you do have a deeper connection, make it easy for your contact to refer you by including in your thank-you/follow-up to this next-job advice conversation a paragraph or two summarizing your achievements and strengths (think of it as a toned-down version of a cover letter that your contact could easily forward to someone who might have a position to fill). Once you see that they've written you a recommendation, be sure to follow up with a thank-you e-mail within a few days and make a point to keep in touch.

In some cases, you might find the roles reversed; your contact might have someone to refer to you, or might end up asking you for insights about your company or career path (either for themselves or on behalf of a mentee or junior staffer on their team). Whenever you can, offer to help, be it with information or by making a referral yourself (but only if you know the person's work well enough to stake your reputation on a recommendation).

HANDLING A JOB SEARCH—WHILE WORKING

You might be wondering how, exactly, you can find the time to spend on revising your résumé, crafting cover letters, searching for job openings, and networking more purposefully when you're already working forty or fifty hours a week (or more) at the job you have. In the early days of your job search, it's really not that hard to find time—it's easy enough to carve out thirty minutes a day to devote to your job search,

OUTSOURCING YOUR RESEARCH

If your job is particularly demanding and truly leaves little time for doing the in-depth research or pre-interview prep necessary for a successful job search, you can pay someone else to do it for you. This doesn't absolve you from studying and understanding the information, but it does save you time for the more strategic parts of your job hunt and interview preparation. Recruiters say outsourcing research is a tactic they're seeing more often, and some say they regularly recommend it to their busier clients.

You can use a site like Elance.com to find a virtual assistant—typically at a cost of $8 to $15 per hour—to pull together basic research on your target companies: things like their size, the location of their headquarters, the names of their most senior executives, their major products or clients, and the most significant news from the last year. This tactic works best if you provide the virtual assistant with a format for how you want to receive the information, limit the person's work to just background and second-level research, and don't try to outsource the thinking that needs to go into your job search. You still need to read through and digest the materials you get and devise your own strategy for approaching the company or preparing for the interview.

If you're searching for a job while still employed, it's generally wise to keep your job hunt quiet until you're ready for people at the office to know you're ready to jump ship. Luckily, it's easy enough to ask networking contacts to meet outside work hours or reserve some time to chat at your next professional association event, but you can also ask for informational meetings and interviews to be held outside of typical work hours, say, over breakfast or at the end of a workday. Many recruiters and hiring managers are open to this since they, too, have packed workdays. In some cases, that kind of flexibility is reserved for candidates seeking more senior positions, but even so, recruiters are usually somewhat sensitive to the intricacies of a job search and will often accommodate a request to schedule an interview for 9 a.m. so your absence from the office is short and gives you a chance to change out of your interview suit into your usual work attire rather than wearing fancy duds to work all of a sudden (which would be awkward and a telltale sign if it isn't your usual work wear).

If you're trying to keep your job search under wraps, it goes without saying that you shouldn't send job inquiries through your work e-mail, update your LinkedIn profile, or fine-tune your résumé while at work. If you need to set up an interview by phone, or are doing phone interviews, schedule these calls during lunch, before work, or during a time when you can leave the office. That might mean sitting in your car for twenty minutes or walking to a park a few blocks away. It's never a smart move to attempt a new-job–related phone call in the office. It's not that Big Brother is tapping your phone calls, but more that these days, office spaces are more cramped—with many companies eschewing actual offices for cubicles or semiwalled (if you can call them walls) officles offering little privacy. Even if you think nobody is around, it's pretty likely someone is within earshot or will walk your way. And your efforts to try to speak quietly are exactly the signal that curious ears perk up for. What's more, trying to hold such a conversation in the office is likely to make you nervous about who will hear you. Nervousness or timidity is not something you want to convey to someone able to pass you from phone interview to in-person candidate.

When the time comes for more intense interviewing, there's no getting around it: you'll probably need to take a personal or vacation day. You may need to take more than one day, particularly if you need to prepare or do significant research before the interview. If one day is all you can manage, try to spread your prep work out over a few evenings and then schedule these interviews for late morning or early afternoon (but not after 3 p.m.; research shows that many interviewers are less tuned in later in the day). Take the whole day off (which is less suspicious anyway) and use the early morning to finish your research on the company and the people you'll be meeting with (check out their bios on the corporate website, LinkedIn, and professional association directories).[36]

and if you work efficiently, that should be all you need. As you progress to the interview stage, however, the process will become more time consuming, so you'll need to get creative—or at least smarter—about your search.

The early step—researching companies and jobs, updating your résumé, and adding accomplishments or an up-to-date photo to LinkedIn or an industry association profile—can be easily done on weekends or at night. Often, you'll find making such updates online will get the recruiting ball rolling. Your profile will begin to turn up when recruiters search for candidates to fill a certain position and, suddenly, your search has come to you (those referrals you asked for and gave in return will also help here).

Professional networking websites are particularly popular with recruiters who have specific needs to fill when hiring. "Eighty-five percent of recruiters use LinkedIn to find talent," Connie Thanasoulis-Cerrachio, a career services expert with Vault.com and a former Fortune 500 recruiter, told *The Wall Street Journal.* "It's a completely passive job search tool." And John Phillips, the director of Global Talent Labs at Microsoft Corp., told the *Journal* that one of the first places his recruiters look is networking sites, LinkedIn in particular, to find candidates.[37]

INTERVIEWING AS AN EXPERIENCED CANDIDATE

When you were in college and interviewing for your first job, you were put through the paces. Your interview questions were more rote and the exercises companies used to judge you were, well, designed to sift through a heap of twenty-two-year-olds who were smart and ambitious but largely unproven. It was less important to show how you could be an asset to a firm. Now that you've had real responsibility, perhaps a promotion, and tangible successes and impact on the bottom line, you've got more to talk about in an interview.

That means you need to adjust your interview style. For most people, this isn't all that difficult. The same basic interview rules (dress professionally, make eye contact, show enthusiasm and energy) still apply and will come more naturally because by now you are used to meeting new people and discussing your accomplishments, and you're more confident in your abilities and candidacy than you were when the world of work was still a bit murky. What's more, you're knee-deep in the industry and understand how your field and function works on its own, across different departments, and in the broader context of a company. It all adds up to much more to say in an interview.

In your résumé you should have a comprehensive list of your achievements distilled to the highlights. When you interview, it's important to get these into the conversation. Offer them as examples when you answer questions or as proof when asked about certain abilities—and relate them to the firm you want to work for. The best way to do that is to develop a strong understanding of the company, its businesses, and its challenges. Websites like GlassDoor.com, Indeed.com, and Vault.com often include common interview questions in profiles of companies that they maintain. Many times, those questions are submitted directly by people who have recently interviewed with the company and are divided by the type of position they were seeking. This is an invaluable resource— and it's free! Read through to get a sense of what you might face in your own interview and prepare to answer those questions. Then practice how you might answer some common questions and some specific to your field.

Finally, as an experienced candidate, you have a lot more room to ask questions and evaluate the employer, too. You should take full advantage of that so you can get a good sense of the culture of the firm, the work style of the team and division you'd be working with and in, the values of the company and its managers, and the opportunities you will have to move up or to take on bigger challenges. Don't be afraid to ask these questions in a direct way. Some possible queries: Does the company promote from within? How is conflict handled within the group? Do people at this level work autonomously, mostly within a team, or a combination of both? What traits would you say describe the people here? How are decisions made in this group? Where did the last person in this role go?

Why ask these sorts of questions? You want to find a job that will have more than just a great title or be with a prestigious company. You also want to work in a firm and with a team whose values, opportunities, and direction are aligned with your own—at least in the areas that matter most to you. So listen carefully to the answers you get and consider what you've heard and what you didn't hear. You'll want to be able to call these things to mind if you get a job offer.

EVALUATING A NEXT-JOB OFFER

For the most part, the way you evaluate a job offer now is similar to the way you considered your first-job offers. But because you were more exacting when choosing the jobs you applied for this time around, and you've moved from applying for wide-swath entry-level jobs toward more specific, skills-and-career-move–based jobs, it's much more likely you'll know the job is a good move for building your professional career before you get an offer. But there are still plenty of things to consider and negotiate once you get an offer, and the process will be different than it was a few years ago. Be sure to do any negotiating over the phone or in person, unless the person making the offer indicates you should do otherwise. E-mail if you must, but follow up with a call.

As you consider an offer, it's time to tap your network once again. You'll want to talk to people who have worked at the company, who currently work there, or who have friends or colleagues who are familiar with the culture and pay structure at the company. If someone like that comes to mind right away, great. Send a note, make contact via LinkedIn, or pick up the phone and ask for a little time to discuss the company (be clear that you are evaluating a job offer and want to get some insight from a person familiar with the company but not directly involved in hiring you).

If you don't personally know someone with a connection to the firm or if the only person you do know is the same person who pushed your candidacy (who is likely to paint a rosier picture because, after all, that person wants you on board and probably gets a bonus of some kind if you do take the job), ask trusted mentors or others in your professional or alumni network if they can point you to someone with inside knowledge. You can also peruse the profiles of your closest contacts on LinkedIn or other professional networking websites to see if they're connected to company insiders and ask for an introduction. Once you've found someone—or better yet, a couple of people—to talk to, here's what to consider and bounce off those contacts:

THE PATH FORWARD

You dig this job. It's got almost everything you were looking for and will really help you build your career. It's not just a stepping-stone . . . or is it? Take a step back and consider where the job is likely to lead next. Where did your would-be manager say the last person in the job went? Where do people in similar jobs at the company or other companies go from here? Once you find out, ask yourself if *these* are the types of jobs you'd like to have a few years down the road, or, if not—gut check time—can you get where you *do* want to go from this position? If you've been attentive to your career path and aspirations, chances are the answer will be yes. But, it's always good to survey what's on the horizon and make sure it matches where you want to be when you get there.

Ask your insider contacts about how people move around at the company and whether that enticing promise you heard from higher-ups about growth from within is a reality or just a nice thought to hook you on the job. Will this position give you the tools, skills, experience, and exposure you need to get where you want to be in three or five years? Sure, it may seem awfully early to be worried about that now, but it's important to start thinking this way—with each step of your career, you need to be thinking about how this job and this work will help you grow. That's what building a professional career is all about—building upon all the skills and experience you achieve as you move your way up the ladder.

THE BOSS AND GROUP CULTURE

What looks like a career-catapulting job can quickly fizzle if the person you work for or the culture of the group is a bad fit, or worse, doesn't allow you to bring your best to the table. This is even truer for more experienced positions, where stakes are higher and office politics are trickier to navigate, than it is for entry-level ones. What's the "right" culture? It really depends on how you work best. Consider the situations in which you've really been able to excel, shine, and grow—and be recognized as a much-needed contributor to the company. Now replay that time in your mind, paying special attention to the culture and supervision that made it possible. Was it high pressure, deadline intensive, but collaborative with a demanding but fair boss? Was it a hands-off situation where you succeeded because the boss left you alone to run with a task? What made things work so well with that boss—or others under whom you've had success? What cultural norms do you think contributed to your ability to really excel?

The boss and culture around the job you've been offered don't need to be an exact match to have the same effect, but you should be able to identify several of the same key elements. And if you think of a time where you didn't meet your potential or strained under a certain boss, consider the behavior and culture that existed in that situation. You should think twice if the job you're offered has several of those same elements as mainstays of the culture or are at the core of your would-be boss's management style. If you're not sure, quiz your insider contacts about how the boss handles disputes, problems, and jobs well done. Ask about the dynamics and traits that make someone successful in the particular group or in working with a particular supervisor. Are these traits you have? Are the dynamics something you can thrive in, even if it means adapting? Remember, you want this job to be more than just a stepping-stone.

BENEFITS

Even if you're a few years into your career, you still won't have much room to negotiate basic benefits like 401(k) contributions or healthcare plans. But you should consider them as part of your overall package. If the company automatically adds $5,000 to your 401(k) account every year—and matches your contributions dollar-for-dollar—that's a very valuable benefit (unless you have something better already) and could compensate for a less-than-hoped-for salary. These benefits may be more important to you now than they were just a few years ago—especially if you're starting or thinking about starting a family—so they should weigh strongly on your decision.

Take a look at the vacation time you are offered. If it's less than you currently have, ask if the company will match your current amount of time off. It's a reasonable request that will often be granted.

SALARY AND BONUS

Now that you're an experienced hire, you'll have more wiggle room for negotiating a salary—something that wasn't always true when you were looking for your first job. But you should make sure you have a sense of what a fair salary is for the job. Again, sites like GlassDoor.com and PayScale.com can be useful. Postings for similar jobs that list a salary range are also useful. And if your professional association conducts salary surveys, you can use those as a benchmark, too. Sometimes a peer who recently landed a similar job can be a good resource for figuring out if the offer you've received is a fair one. You can also ask your insider contact for a sense of the salary ranges for positions like the one you've been offered. But unless you trust the person implicitly, it's probably best not to specify the exact salary and bonus you've been offered.

If you find there's room to ask for more and believe it's warranted based on the job itself (regardless of the salary you're earning now, particularly if you are underpaid), the old adage about taking a new job being the best way to get a big salary increase generally holds true. The rule of thumb for moving to a new position that's a notch up from the one you have is a minimum 10 percent increase in base pay. If you're moving from a staff role to a leadership role in which you'll manage others, expect—or negotiate for—something closer to 15 percent to 20 percent. If you have a bonus target, it should be equal to or better than the target in your current job.

In some cases, you'll have an easier time negotiating for a bigger bonus target than a bigger salary; that's a cultural question to ask an insider. If the company making the offer is in a hurry to fill the position, you'll probably have more wiggle room to get a better salary and bonus than the initial offer. If the cost of, say, healthcare premiums for employees is significantly higher than what you pay now, you might also be able to use that to get a bump in the salary you're offered. Negotiating a better salary might seem somewhat trivial if you've found a dream job or if you have few expenses to worry about. But what you earn now will impact your earnings (and every other chance you have to negotiate) exponentially for years to come, when it will matter.

NEXT THINGS NEXT

Once you've negotiated your offer and asked for an official offer letter (and in some cases, signed and returned it) for a new position, it's time to submit an official resignation to your current boss. You need to do this politely and respectfully, even if you despise your current job. You don't want to burn bridges with your peers and supervisors; you're bound to run into them again someday if you stay in the field long enough. When you explain that you are leaving, thank your boss and any key colleagues or managers for the experience and time they've dedicated to helping you grow as a professional.

Your official resignation letter should be professional in tone and should offer at least two weeks' notice—more if you're in the midst of a big project that doesn't end for, say, three or four weeks. You should also offer to leave instructions for anything that you'll need to pass off to someone else. In some industries, the company you are leaving won't want you to serve out those last weeks, particularly if you're leaving for a job with a rival firm. But you should always offer. Consider sending a personal handwritten note of thanks to colleagues or mentors who were particularly helpful in this first job—and whom you want to stay in touch with as you progress in your career. No sappiness needed, just a genuine thanks for taking an interest and a mention of a specific detail or two about why you appreciate the person's efforts.

When you start your new job, you'll probably feel some of the same newbie anxieties you did just a few years before. But this time, you'll know where to look for information, the kinds of people to turn to for guidance, and how to adapt and perform in any number of situations. What's more, you'll have less to prove about what you know (note, that doesn't say *nothing* to prove, just less) because you have several years of solid experience and proof of your abilities under your belt.

It's not time to rest, of course. This is just your second job, albeit one of the more important steps in your career. Approach it with the same dedication and drive as you did your first job out of college. And don't pull back on involvement in professional associations, continued education, pursuit of certifications, or the occasional networking breakfast. Those are some of the very things that helped you get from point A to point B—and they'll help you get to points C, D, and E, too. Your involvement, educational needs, and mentoring relationships will evolve as you get more experience and you're likely to be a mentor to someone else soon or find yourself tapped to lead that industry association committee, not just be a member of it. Take advantage of these opportunities the same way other professionals you want to emulate have taken advantage.

And, of course, when a twenty-two-year-old whiz-kid college graduate lands a spot on your team, remember what it was like to be in that spot and do what you can to help him along. Consider it both a bit of paying it forward and an insurance policy of sorts. After all, you might want to work for that guy one day.

ACKNOWLEDGMENTS

Special thanks go to the people who helped me craft and research this book, especially Sarah E. Needleman, Erin White, and Elizabeth Garone, staff reporters and freelancer at *The Wall Street Journal*; Teri Evans, Joe Walker, Marisa Taylor, and a host of others who helped produce the *WSJ* Best Colleges ranking; the bloggers of *WSJ*'s Laid Off and Looking and Hire Education blogs; the bright researchers at QuintCareers .com; and the countless recruiters, college career service professionals, and young graduates and recent interns whose experiences helped shape this book.

Rose Ellen D'Angelo at *The Wall Street Journal* and Talia Krohn helped guide me from proposal to finished pages. Both were supportive as I changed jobs, missed some deadlines, and reworked supporting materials. Thanks to Mark Birkey and Andrea Peabbles, whose smart copyediting and proofing made the text flow well and read clean.

My two children, Cullen and Lila, and my husband, Keith Slattery, supported this effort, vacating the house for hours at a time so I could write. My in-laws, Loretta and Hank Slattery, and babysitters Ashley Hallmark and Tina DelPurgatorio also pitched in to watch the children while I scrambled to finish chapters.

The idea for this book was born out of my own love of helping young people build their careers and from watching

Ashley and other young college grads and interns struggle to figure out the magic formula for building the foundation for a professional career. It's the special sauce so
many people want, yet it remains elusive. Not anymore, I
hope.

NOTES

1. Bernard Haldane, PhD, "Dependable Strengths Project," presentation paper, College of Education, University of Washington, 1989.
2. University of California–Berkeley's Peer Corner, http://careercenter peers.typepad.com/my_weblog/.
3. Shalini Sharan, "What Am I Missing?" *The Wall Street Journal*, Hire Education Blog, November 4, 2010, http://blogs.wsj.com/hire-education/ 2010/11/04/what-am-i-missing/.
4. Ashley Starks, "An Externship Proves Pivotal," *The Wall Street Journal*, Hire Education Blog, December 9, 2010, http://blogs.wsj.com/ hire-education/2010/12/09/an-externship-proves-pivotal/.
5. Alexandra Cheney, "Firms Assess Young Interns' Potential," *The Wall Street Journal*, September 13, 2010, http://online.wsj.com/article/SB100 01424052748704206804575467914217160480.html.
6. National Association of Colleges and Employers, 2010 Internship Survey, http://www.naceweb.org/Infographics/2011_Internship_Survey.aspx.
7. Jennifer Merritt, Teri Evans, Alexandra Cheney, et al., "Paths to Professions Project," *The Wall Street Journal*, September 13, 2010, http://online .wsj.com/public/page/rankings-career-college-majors.html.
8. National Association of Colleges and Employers, 2010 Student Benchmarking Survey Research Brief, http://www.naceweb.org/Products/ 2010_Student_Survey.aspx.
9. Jonnelle Marte, "Creating Internships Out of Thin Air," *The Wall Street Journal*, May 18, 2010, http://online.wsj.com/article/SB1000142405274 8703460404575244903412880836.html.
10. Victoria E. Knight, "Tapping Talent Through Internship Programs," *The Wall Street Journal*, August 24, 2009, http://online.wsj.com/article/ SB125112170997753771.html.
11. Starks, "An Externship Proves Pivotal."
12. Goldman Sachs Summer Intern Toolkit, "Dos and Don'ts," Goldman Sachs career portal, http://www2.goldmansachs.com/careers/begin/ summer-intern-toolkit/index.html.
13. Lindsey Pollak, *Getting from College to Career* (New York: Harper Paperback, 2007).
14. Emily Noonan, "A Word to the Awkward: Networking Takes Practice," *The Wall Street Journal*, Hire Education Blog, October 27, 2010, http:// blogs.wsj.com/hire-education/2010/10/27/a-word-to-the-awkward -networking-takes-practice/.

15. Teri Evans, "Penn State Tops Recruiter Rankings," *The Wall Street Journal*, September 13, 2010, http://online.wsj.com/article/SB10001424052748 70435890457547764336966352.html.

16. Teri Evans, "Research Agreements Play Big Role in Jobs," *The Wall Street Journal*, September 13, 2010, http://online.wsj.com/article/SB1000142 40527487038972045754880508943447786.html.

17. Ibid.

18. Joe Walker, "Firms Invest Big in Career Sites," *The Wall Street Journal*, June 8, 2010, http://online.wsj.com/article/SB1000142405274870476440457528725424958802.html.

19. Potentialpark Communications, "Top Career Websites 2010," http://www.potentialpark.com/teweb-ranking-2010/.

20. Bain & Company, "How to Ace the Case Interview," http://www.bain.com/bainweb/pdfs/acethecase.pdf.

21. McKinsey & Company, "Techniques and Tricks," http://www.mckinsey.com/careers/how_do_i_apply/how_to_do_well_in_the_interview/case_interview/techniques_and_tricks.aspx.

22. Ken Sundheim, "Graduate Salary Negotiations," KAS Placement, http://www.kasplacement.com.

23. Randall S. Hansen, PhD, and Katharine Hansen, PhD, "Your First Days Working at a New Job: 20 Tips to Help You Make a Great Impression," Quintessential Careers, http://www.quintcareers.com/first_days_working.html.

24. Erin White, "The First Job Blues: How to Adjust, When to Move On," *The Wall Street Journal*, July 25, 2006.

25. Erin White, "Phone Tips for Newbies," *The Wall Street Journal*, August 2005.

26. Toddi Gutner, "Ways to Make the Most of a Negative Job Review," *The Wall Street Journal*, January 13, 2009, http://online.wsj.com/article/SB123180183720875181.html.

27. Elizabeth Garone, "When You Dislike Your Assigned Mentor," *The Wall Street Journal*, August 27, 2009, http://online.wsj.com/article/SB125106050374252091.html.

28. Toddi Gutner, "Finding Anchors in the Storm: Mentors," *The Wall Street Journal*, January 27, 2009, http://online.wsj.com/article/SB123301451869117603.html.

29. Erin White, "Making Mentorships Work—Building Trust, Setting Guidelines Are Key to Successful Programs," *The Wall Street Journal*, October 23, 2007, http://online.wsj.com/article/SB119310906855868119.html.

30. Katherine Hansen, PhD, "The Value of a Mentor," Quintessential Careers, http://www.quintcareers.com/mentor_value.html.

31. Sarah E. Needleman, "Giving Time Off for Good Behavior," *The Wall Street Journal*, December 2, 2008, http://online.wsj.com/article/SB122764965722957617.html.

32. Elizabeth Garone, "Planning a Move to Your Second Job," *The Wall Street Journal*, February 25, 2008, http://online.wsj.com/article/SB120369362609685909.html.

33. Careerbuilder.com, "Forty-five Percent of Employers Use Social Networking Sites to Research Job Candidates, CareerBuilder Survey Finds," August 19, 2009, http://www.careerbuilder.com/share/aboutus/pressreleasesdetail.aspx?id=pr519&sd=8%2F19%2F2009&ed=12%2F31%2F2009.

34. Mark S. Granovetter, *Getting a Job: A Study of Contacts and Careers*, 2nd edition (Chicago: University of Chicago Press, 1995).
35. Jason Alba, "Asking for LinkedIn Recommendations—Is That Okay?," I'm on LinkedIn, Now What blog, November 24, 2008, http://imon linkedinnowwhat.com/2008/11/24/asking-for-linkedin-recommen dations-is-that-okay/.
36. Elizabeth Garone, "Job Hunting Under the Boss's Nose," *The Wall Street Journal*, June 22, 2010, http://online.wsj.com/article/SB100014240527 48704895204575320953473841156.html.
37. Ibid.

INDEX

ABOUT THE AUTHOR

Jennifer Merritt was Careers editor for *The Wall Street Journal* and WSJ.com until March of 2011. She has been involved in covering or editing stories about professional careers and career choices for the better part of the last decade.

In 2008, Jennifer developed the *Journal*'s "Second Acts" feature—a regular column that looks at real people and the challenges and outcomes to their career changes. The same year, Jennifer also developed "90 Days," a regular instructive column that offers sound advice for tackling the first ninety days of any career change.

In 2009, Jennifer developed the blog Laid Off and Looking, chronicling the job searches of laid-off professionals. A year later, the blog Hire Education debuted, chronicling the job searches of college seniors. Jennifer also managed the *Journal*'s business school–related rankings projects and management education coverage.

Jennifer is currently the Wealth Management editor at Thomson Reuters, where she manages a staff of reporters and editors covering the money management business, from financial advisors to the inner workings of big brokerage firms to the career moves and developments in the wealth management industry.

Before joining the *Journal*, Jennifer was an editor at *Money* magazine, overseeing the magazine's projects, including "Best Places to Live" and "Best Jobs." Jennifer also served as business editor at the *Florida Times-Union* in Jacksonville, Florida, and spent five years as an editor and writer at *BusinessWeek,* overseeing the magazine's management education coverage and rankings projects. She is co-author of several books, including three editions of *BusinessWeek*'s *Guide to the Best Business Schools* and *Making Allowances,* all published by McGraw-Hill. Prior to these roles, Jennifer was a reporter in Boston and Florida.

As Careers editor, Jennifer regularly appeared on CNN's *Your Money and Your Bottom Line,* discussing career trends and offering career advice. She has also appeared on *Good Morning America,* Fox News, and local network affiliates to speak on career and education-related topics.

While at the *Florida Times-Union,* the section Jennifer edited received honorable mention in SABEW's Best in Business Award for best business section. Jennifer is also the recipient of Northwestern University's first-ever Young Alumni Emerging Leader Award (2003). She received a bachelor's degree in journalism from the school and was part of a team of former students whose reporting, after five years of work, helped provide the evidence needed to exonerate a wrongfully convicted death-row inmate.

Jennifer lives in the New York City suburbs with her husband and two children.